RAW FOOD
RECIPES&PREPARATION

Saskia Fraser is a raw food expert, author and lifestyle coach. She has helped thousands of busy working women to experience greater energy, mental clarity and self-confidence. Saskia runs raw food detoxes and workshops, in-person and online, as well as one-to-one life-coaching programmes. She is the author of *Raw Freedom*, a raw food recipe book for busy lives, as well as a popular raw food blog.

Publisher & Creative Director: Nick Wells
Senior Project Editor: Catherine Taylor
Copy Editor: Kathy Steer
Art Director: Mike Spender
Layout Design: Jane Ashley
Digital Design & Production: Chris Herbert
Proofreader: Dawn Laker

Special thanks to Gillian Whitaker

FLAME TREE PUBLISHING
6 Melbray Mews, Fulham,
London SW6 3NS, United Kingdom
www.flametreepublishing.com

This edition published 2016

Copyright © 2016 Flame Tree Publishing Ltd

16 18 19 17 15
1 3 5 7 9 10 8 6 4 2

ISBN: 978-1-78361-992-4

Picture Credits
TurboBlend® VS © Vitamix®: 69tr; ©2016 KitchenAid: 72l. © StockFood and the following: 25l Cölfen, Elisabeth; 33br Gräfe & Unzer Verlag / Zanin, Melanie; 64r Johnér; 69b Campbell, Ryla; 78r Vaquer, Haidee; 82tl Strokin, Yelena; 111 Gräfe & Unzer Verlag / Lang, Coco; 155 Baranowski, Andre; 159 & front cover PhotoCuisine / Belmonte, Laurent; 184 PhotoCuisine / Desgrieux. Courtesy Shutterstock.com and the following: 1, 43t Nitr; 3, 66t, 219 zstock; 4 Malyugin; 6l Piotr Adamowicz; 6r SunKids; 7l, 194 Anna_Pustynnikova; 7r Zju4ka; 9 Lisa Kolbasa; 13b, 44tr Dream79; 13tr Elena Shashkina; 13tl Lucky_elephant; 14, 73r Anna Hoychuk; 16l goodluz; 16r Kite_rin; 17l, 43bl, 44bl, 78l, 81r, 89 Brent Hofacker; 17r Maria Shumova; 19 mongione; 20 JoannaTkaczuk; 23br, 163 Kati Molin; 23bl l i g h t p o e t; 23t StockLite; 24l, 48r Africa Studio; 24r Karaidel; 25r pilipphoto; 27, 49l Stephanie Frey; 28r ALINAT17; 28l TheX; 29l Bukhta Yurii; 29r, 55tr, 97 Magdalena Paluchowska; 30 Ilya Andriyanov; 33t Monkey Business Images; 33bl Wichy; 34r, 58tr, 104, 107, 137, 189 sarsmis; 34l, 207 Vorontsova Anastasiia; 35r mama_mia; 35r otarikokojevs; 37 saschanti17; 38br grafvision; 38bl Oksana Mizina; 38t Valentyn Volkov; 40–41 leonori; 43br racorn; 44br Malivan_Iuliia; 44tl Timmary; 47 baibaz; 48l, 79l Ildi Papp; 49r, 82bl AS Food studio; 51bl 135pixels; 51t 5PH; 51br, 91, 157, 216 Elena Veselova; 52 Ievgeniia Maslovska; 55b id-art; 55tl merc67; 57 Adisa; 58tl Igor S. Srdanovic; 58b, 85tl Luna Vandoorne; 60–61 5 second Studio; 63 Phoenixns; 64l dianaduda; 65r Alliance; 65l Charles B. Ming Onn; 66bl, 66br violeta pasat; 69tl NinaM; 70 –71 AnastasiaKopa; 72r Natasha Breen; 73l Sergiy Bykhunenko; 74 –75 13Smile; 77 Andy Dean Photography; 79r Syda Productions; 80r Alena Haurylik; 80l Chamille White; 81l Diana Taliun; 82br, 82tr riggsby; 85tr Agnes Kantaruk; 85b Deymos.HR; 92 Pikoso.kz; 94–95 Aleksandrova Karina; 99 A_Lein; 101 Geshas; 108–109 casanisa; 113 ILEISH ANNA; 116 Olga_Phoenix; 119, 121, 177, 199 Magdanatka; 122 NADKI; 124–125 lidante; 127, 145 dashkin14; 129 denio109; 130 Aleksandra Kovac; 133 ISchmidt; 139, 181, 183 phoelix; 141 Ekaterina Bratova; 142–143 Stepanek Photography; 147 Andi Berger; 148 Anna Ewa Bieniek; 151 AlenaKogotkova; 160, 164–165 Zaira Zarotti; 167 Alexey Borodin; 169, 208 Elena M. Tarasova; 170 Lilyana Vynogradova; 173 manukahoto; 179 Rohit Seth; 191 Marykkin; 201, 213, 215 Nataliya Arzamasova; 202 Edith Frincu; 205 Alena Ozerova; 211 Igabriela; 221 loveofphoto.

RAW FOOD
RECIPES & PREPARATION

Saskia Fraser

FLAME TREE
PUBLISHING

CONTENTS

INTRODUCTION

I n recent years raw food has risen in popularity. Not only is it delicious, but the health and wellbeing benefits are undeniable for anyone choosing to introduce more raw food into their diet. Increased energy, weight loss, improved sleep and emotional balance are a few of the effects that you can look forward to experiencing.

HOW TO USE THIS BOOK

This book is here to guide and inspire you on your discovery of the delicious and exciting world of raw food. It can feel a little daunting at first. What is raw food? Which foods are considered raw and which are not? What does a raw food diet consist of? These questions and more are covered in the section What is Raw? (*see* pages 12–21).

Raw food is not a diet in the traditional sense; it is a lifestyle choice that enhances how you feel physically, mentally and emotionally.

There are many positive health benefits in eating a diet high in raw foods. Find out more in the section Why Raw? (*see* pages 22–31).

There is no need to eat 100 per cent raw food in order to experience the benefits of this healthy way of eating. Guidelines on choosing how much raw food to incorporate into your diet, taking into consideration your desired outcomes, are given in the section Making the Transition (*see* pages 32–39).

You may think your options will be limited when eating raw, but you'd be surprised how many delicious foods you can still enjoy – from the obvious fresh fruit and vegetables to sprouted seeds and legumes, nuts, seeds, grains and a whole host of superfoods. These are all described in the section on Raw Food Ingredients (*see* pages 42–57).

Knowing what equipment you need and how to use it is the starting point for setting up your raw-friendly kitchen. Find out about the gadgets and raw equipment that will help take your raw experience to the next level in our section Tools and Equipment (*see* pages 59–73).

When it comes to making raw recipes, preparation techniques are simple but varied. The section on Preparation and Techniques (*see* pages 76–84) will teach you how to make raw food prep simple and quick. Get ready to feel confident and excited about making satisfying and delicious raw food.

THE RECIPES

The raw recipes in the following pages have been created with everyday life in mind. Simple smoothies, quick breakfasts, lunches and snacks are the mainstay of a raw diet, and there is a chapter dedicated to staple raw recipes. With these mainstays under your belt, healthy raw eating becomes not only tasty but easy and fuss-free too.

The weekend is the time to get creative with more complicated recipes that take a little bit longer, but when raw cheesecake, crackers or quiche are the result you will see that they are well worth the effort. Prepare to be amazed!

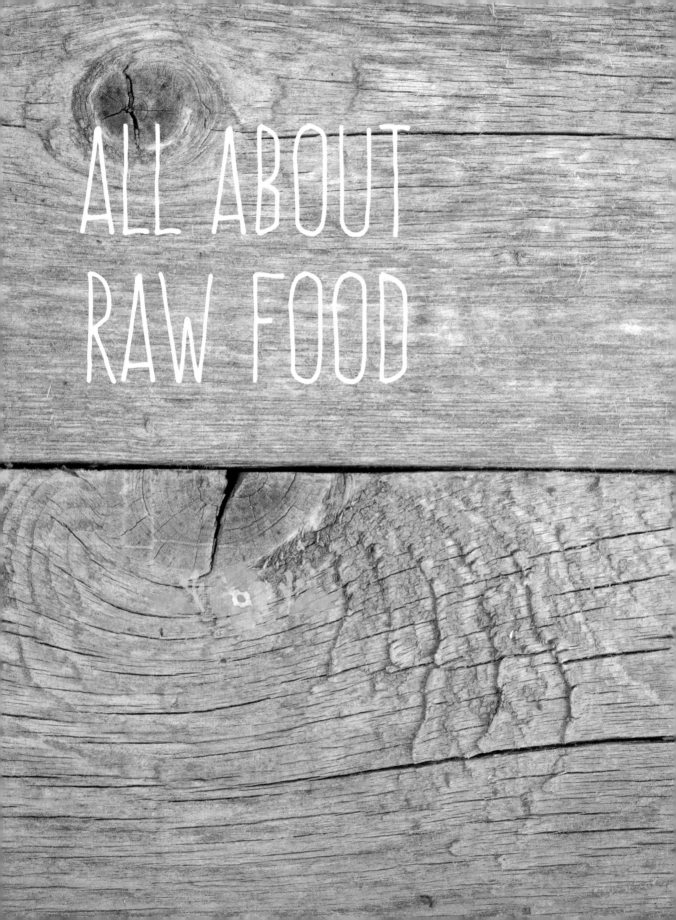

ALL ABOUT
RAW FOOD

WHAT IS RAW?

A BRIEF HISTORY OF RAW FOOD

Raw food has undoubtedly seen a huge surge in popularity in recent years, but people have actually been eating raw since ancient times. Cooked food became the norm after the discovery of fire, but before then our ancestors survived on a purely raw diet.

The Raw Food Movement

In the 1930s, Dr Paul Kouchakoff M.D., discovered that eating cooked food did in fact cause a toxic reaction in the body. He also found that this toxic response was completely absent when plant-based foods were eaten in their raw state. Despite this discovery, raw food was only discussed and explored by a select few.

Raw food started to become part of the mainstream consciousness in the 1970s. Viktoras Kulvinskas's (b. 1939) book *Survival into the 21st Century* explored the benefits of eating living foods, demonstrating how raw food and holistic living can transform health. It was the first raw food guide available to help people achieve optimum nutrition, mental clarity and vibrant health through their diet.

A Modern Phenomenon

When Juliano Brotman's (b. 1970) *Raw: The UNcook Book*, was released in 1999, raw food started to become popularized and more accessible to the everyday person. Today, raw food is becoming increasingly accepted as part of mainstream culture, with smoothies, fresh green juices and spiralized vegetables available in supermarkets.

RAW FOOD DEFINED

People are often unsure what raw food actually is. Raw recipes are taste-bud sensations to rival any cooked dish. Such delights as nut cheese, fresh and lively soups, healthy chocolate cake, rich and creamy seed milks and much more await you when you dive into the world of raw food.

Uncooked

The simplest definition of raw food is 'uncooked whole foods'. The vast majority of fruit and vegetables are edible raw, including less obvious candidates such as sweet potatoes, aubergine (eggplant) and rhubarb. Other foods that come under the heading of 'raw food' include many whole grains, sprouted pulses, seaweeds, nuts, seeds and superfoods.

Sun-baked

A common misconception is that raw food is uncooked and therefore cold. Raw food can actually be slowly warmed to 45°C/113°F. Raw foods below this temperature maintain the majority of their nutrients, but heating raw foods above this temperature begins to destroy valuable vitamins, minerals and plant-based phytonutrients.

The gentle heating of raw foods to 45°C/113°F can be used to warm recipes, such as raw soups and raw sauces. It can also be used to slowly dehydrate ingredients while maintaining their nutrients. In this way, you can make storecupboard goods, such as raw crackers and dried fruits and vegetables, as well as fruit leathers (a puréed fruit snack) using a dehydrating machine.

HOW MUCH RAW FOOD IS RIGHT FOR YOU?

Embracing a raw diet is not about eating 100 per cent raw food. There are different ways of integrating raw food into your life, depending on what you want to achieve through this way of eating. Do you want better health? More energy? Weight loss? Or all three?

Cleansing

Eating raw food is naturally cleansing and detoxifying for your body. The more raw food you eat, the more strongly you will cleanse. How toxic your system is, from years of a less-than-optimal diet and lifestyle, will influence how strongly you feel the effects of this detox.

For gentle cleansing, it is advisable to introduce raw foods gradually, as you reduce the more toxic foods in your diet.

Eating lots of raw food immediately will produce a strong detox. Although this can be an uncomfortable experience, it may be one you find necessary for health reasons. It is important to support your body through a strong detox with supplementary cleansing activities, such as drinking lots of water, exercise, enemas, breathing exercises and meditation.

A Matter of Degree

The amount of raw food that someone includes in their diet is often referred to in degrees, e.g. a 75-per-cent raw food diet or 100-per-cent raw food diet. A 75-per-cent raw food diet includes approximately 75 per cent raw food and 25 per cent cooked food, while a 100-per-cent raw food diet is a diet that contains only raw foods.

The more raw food you eat, the healthier and more energized you will feel. However, for your mental and emotional health, you may find it valuable to maintain a less rigid mindset by incorporating elements of cooked eating.

Lifestyle Balance

It is important to take your lifestyle into consideration when deciding how much raw food to eat. Some people are ready for a radically healthy lifestyle change, while others simply want to take their healthy eating to the next level.

If you want to eat out and share meals with friends without compromising, then aim for a percentage of raw that takes this into account, such as 50–75 per cent. If you are prepared to order off-menu in restaurants, asking for something raw, and to share your delicious raw meals with friends, then you can increase the percentage to 90–100 per cent.

THE ETHICS OF RAW FOOD

If the idea of eating raw food appeals to you it is likely that you are also conscious of your contribution to the health of our planet. Eating a diet high in raw food is one way of contributing to the Earth's wellbeing.

Raw Food & Veganism

A raw food diet is usually mostly, if not all, vegan. There is growing evidence that a mostly vegan diet is far better for our health and the planet than a meat-based diet.

The vast majority of raw food is naturally animal-free. It is possible to eat raw fish, dried and fresh raw meat, raw egg and unpasteurized cheese and dairy products. However, most people following a raw food diet tend to avoid these foods for a number of health reasons:

- Animal products leave behind an acid ash in the body after digestion, adding to the health-depleting condition of over-acidity (linked to such conditions as arthritis and cancer).
- Raw animal products contain far more parasites and microbes than plant-based foods.
- Animal products tend to be energy-heavy when it comes to digestion.

Non-vegan ingredients common in the raw food diet include bee products, such as honey and bee pollen. Some people also like to include cooked eggs and unpasteurized cheese into their high raw food diet.

The Importance of Organic

Non-organic foods contain traces of agrochemicals that, when eaten, can remain in the body and possibly contribute to health issues. There is evidence that these chemicals remain in the body after digestion. Traces of herbicides and pesticides have been found in mothers' milk and human fat tissue. If you are eating non-organic food, you are also ingesting traces of these agrochemicals. Unfortunately you cannot remove all these toxic traces simply by washing your food, so eating more organic products will reduce your exposure to these potentially harmful chemicals.

Food Miles

Eating raw food gives you the opportunity to lessen your food miles, reducing the impact of what you eat on the planet. In the spring and summer months, fresh, local produce is becoming more widely available through farmers' markets, box schemes and local initiatives.

In the autumn and winter months, although you will probably have to supplement with imported foods, looking for local fresh produce will keep you in touch with the seasons and expand your experience. Pumpkin, parsnips and winter cabbage, to name but a few, are all delicious raw.

WHY RAW?

HEALTH, ENERGY & WELLBEING

It is the desire to feel physically better – more energized, healthier, slimmer – that motivates most people to embrace a high raw food diet. Eating a diet high in raw foods often gives people a sense of energy and wellbeing that they have not experienced for many years, if ever.

Physical Health Benefits

Physical benefits that are common when you eat this way include an energy boost, easy digestion, relief from aching joints and muscle pain, remission of health issues, improved sleep, weight loss, healthier hair and younger-looking skin.

Mental & Emotional Health Benefits

It seems obvious that improving your diet will improve how you feel physically. Surprisingly most people also find that eating raw food has a large impact on their mental and emotional wellbeing too. It is usual to feel calmer, less stressed, happier, more patient and clearer of mind, with improved memory, when you clean up your diet in this way.

Weight Loss

Raw foods, particularly fresh fruits and vegetables, are generally easier for the body to process and assimilate. Eating a high raw food diet is a healthy way to achieve long-term weight loss. Not only do you feel amazing eating this way, but you look better too. People notice that their skin tone improves and that water retention is dramatically reduced.

The Cleansing Effects of Eating Raw

The vast majority of raw foods are naturally detoxifying. When eating this way, you naturally increase the amount of cleansing, water-rich foods that you are taking into your body. Fresh fruits and vegetables, particularly water-rich fruits and dark green leafy vegetables, have a very cleansing effect on the body.

You also naturally decrease many of the more harmful foods that have probably been part of your regular diet. This is one of the major reasons people generally feel so much happier and healthier when they include raw food in their diet.

Alkalizing Your System

Over-acidity in the body has been linked to many of the top health issues in our culture, including heart disease and cancer. Foods such as meat, dairy products, white grains, potatoes, prepackaged fruit juices, foods containing refined sugars, flours and fats,

such as fizzy drinks (sodas), sweets (candies), cakes, coffee and tea, crisps (potato chips), bread and fried foods all contribute to an over-acidic body.

Reducing these acidic foods and increasing the alkalizing foods we eat is incredibly important to long-term health and wellbeing. Many of the ingredients used in a raw diet are naturally alkalising, so help to balance the pH of your system.

A NUTRITIONAL FLOOD

The major reason raw food is so fantastic is because of its nutritional content. The process of cooking food destroys many of the fragile vitamins, enzymes and phytonutrients present in raw foods.

When you eat fresh, raw foods these nutrients are still intact and bioavailable – they are easy for your body to absorb. The more raw foods you include in your diet, the

more your body is flooded with these essential nutrients, which in turn increases your energy, health and overall sense of wellbeing.

Clean Food

When you increase the amount of raw food you eat, you naturally decrease the amount of less healthy food you consume. When you replace your mid-morning cookie or cake with a raw treat; when you replace cow's milk with fresh nut milk; when you eat a fresh raw soup with raw crackers instead of a cooked soup with bread, you are reducing the number of energy-depleting ingredients in your diet.

For ultimate wellbeing the foods to focus on eliminating or reducing include dairy products (such as milk and cheese), wheat and refined sugar products (such as chocolate, bread, cakes, sweets/candies), fried foods, such as takeaways and chips (fries), caffeine (in tea, coffee and 'energy' drinks), alcohol, meat and fish.

Digestion

Digestive load is the term used to describe how much energy your body channels into digesting the food you eat.

Think about when you eat a large, carbohydrate- and animal protein-rich meal, such as a Sunday roast. It is common to feel sluggish and tired after a meal like this, because so much of your body's energy is being channelled into digesting the food you have just eaten.

When you eat fewer cooked foods and increase the amount of raw foods in your diet, this lightens the load on your digestive system. Your energy, instead of being used on heavy digestion of cooked foods, can be used to regenerate and heal your cells and to provide you with a fresh boost

of physical energy. After eating a high raw meal, it is usual to experience an increase in physical energy and brain function. Your health is improving.

Acidifying foods such as sugar, gluten, meat and dairy can also cause inflammation in the gut. Many people experience an improvement in digestive issues when they change their diet to high raw. The alkalising effects of raw food calm and soothe your digestive tract.

Raw foods are also naturally high in healthy fibre, which aids elimination and gut cleansing.

Blood Sugar Balance

The standard diet includes many foods that artificially boost blood sugar. Artificially boosting your blood sugar with sugar or caffeine delivers a

temporary reprieve from tiredness, but is usually followed by an energy dip that requires another artificial boost through more unhealthy snacks or caffeine.

Ingesting these sugary carbohydrate-rich foods and caffeinated drinks causes radical impairment to your body's natural ability to regulate its own blood sugar. A blood sugar imbalance, called hypoglycaemia, causes moodiness, exhaustion, fuzzy-headedness and irritability. It contributes to feelings of stress and lack of confidence in your mental ability. Long term, it can lead to health conditions such as Type 2 diabetes and heart disease.

When you stop managing your energy artificially and start eating a high raw and naturally energizing diet, it can help balance your blood sugar levels. This in turn balances your emotions and helps you to maintain a consistent and positive energy throughout the whole day.

The first step is to wean yourself off sugar and caffeine by gradually reducing your daily intake of tea or coffee and exchanging sugary snacks for fresh fruit or raw snacks. You will notice how your energy begins to stabilize.

Water

Dehydration is another major contributing factor to lack of energy and health issues. We need water in order to maintain healthy cells, to cleanse and to stay hydrated.

Cooking fresh fruits and vegetables actually depletes their water content. When eaten raw, fresh fruits and vegetables have the ability to rehydrate your body more efficiently than a glass of water.

Next time you feel tired, try drinking a big glass of water or eating a couple of fresh, juicy oranges instead of reaching for the coffee or chocolate. You will be amazed at how energising simply rehydrating can be.

MAKING THE TRANSITION

A LIFESTYLE NOT A DIET

Making the transition to a high raw food diet can be daunting, exciting or both. Most people come to raw food because they want to feel healthier and happier, long term. As you introduce more raw food into your life, it is important to remember that it is not a diet in the traditional sense. There is no end point at which you have 'succeeded' or 'failed'.

Eating raw food is a lifestyle choice, one which you will be choosing each day, hopefully for the rest of your life. In the same way you choose what time to get up each day, you will choose to fill your refrigerator with fresh fruits and vegetables. In the same way you decide that a piece of clothing or a piece of equipment no longer suits you or is outdated, you may well decide that coffee, chocolate and a glass of wine in the evening are no longer your go-to 'treats'.

Your fresh and up-to-date lifestyle will include daily treats such as smoothies, raw lime cheesecake (*see* page 202) and nut cheese on sun-dried tomato crackers. Your raw lifestyle will energize and fulfil your body, mind and spirit more than any fully cooked lifestyle can.

AIMS & INSPIRATION

As you get ready to transition to your new raw-inspired lifestyle, it is important to be clear about your aims. Letting go of old dietary habits can be a challenge at first, so this will help you to focus and stay inspired.

Getting Clear

Why are you transitioning to a high raw diet? Spend some time thinking about this question in detail. Think about the physical, emotional, mental and spiritual benefits that are motivating you to upgrade your lifestyle to a raw one. Writing a journal can be a good way of keeping your motivation high.

Keeping Motivated

Inspiration plays a key part in the success of transitioning to a high raw lifestyle long term.

- Inspiring recipes
- Inspiring success stories
- Inspiring teachers
- Inspiring experts
- Inspiring books
- Inspiring personal connections

GENTLY DOES IT

In the beginning, it is tempting to go all-out in the quest to feel the raw 'high'. Some people choose to change their diets to 100 per cent raw overnight, but most people find it far kinder, easier and more rewarding to go gently at first. Your body will start to cleanse and detoxify its cells from the moment you stop eating certain toxic foods and introduce more raw food into your diet.

Recommended Raw Transition Steps

STEP 1

Start by adding a large green smoothie or juice a day, in the morning, afternoon or in the early evening. This will boost your energy and help to gently cleanse your system.

Reduce your intake of refined sugar products, wheat products, dairy products, caffeine, alcohol, fried foods and meat. Replace with raw and healthy substitutes.

Drink 2–3 litres/3½-5 pints/8½-12⅔ cups water each day, to help flush toxins out of your body as you cleanse.

When you feel comfortable with Step 1…

STEP 2

Add in a high raw breakfast each day.

Include at least one raw dish with your midday or evening meal.

Continue reducing refined sugar products, wheat products, dairy products, caffeine, alcohol, fried foods and meat.

When you feel comfortable with Step 2…

STEP 3

Make either your midday or evening meal at least 75 per cent raw.

Eliminate any remaining daily habits that include refined sugar products, wheat products, dairy products, caffeine, alcohol, fried foods and meat.

(Optional) When you feel comfortable with Step 3…

STEP 4

Make both your midday and evening meals at least 75 per cent raw.

Eliminate all refined sugar products, wheat products, dairy products, caffeine, alcohol, fried foods and meat.

GETTING THE RIGHT NUTRIENTS

When you eat a balanced high raw diet, your nutrient intake will generally be much higher than when you are eating a standard diet. A balanced raw food diet includes, most importantly, lots of fresh fruit and vegetables, particularly dark green leafy vegetables in the form of smoothies, soups and salads. Other important sources of essential nutrients include sprouted seeds and pulses, nuts, cold-pressed seed oils such as flaxseed and hemp, seaweeds and algae.

At the beginning, it is easy to lean on nuts and dried fruit as a quick and healthy source of filling food. Initially, these can be a good source of transition food. In the long term, however, eating too many nuts, which are heavy on the digestion, and dried fruits, which are very high in fruit sugar, can deplete your energy and cause weight gain. It is important to use nuts and dried fruit only as light snacks or for 'treat' recipes, rather than relying on them for everyday meals.

If you are vegan, it is important to supplement with vitamin B12. It is not possible to find this nutrient in plant-based wholefoods. If you are concerned about whether you need to supplement with other vitamins and minerals, please see a professional nutritionist.

RAW FOOD INGREDIENTS

FRESH

Fresh fruits and vegetables are the staple elements of the raw food diet. The visual beauty of raw food, evident in the vibrant colours of the ingredients, is more than merely aesthetic.

Eat the Rainbow

The different colours present in fruits and vegetables illustrate their different nutritional qualities and eating a rainbow of fresh fruit and vegetables will give you a wide range of these life-giving nutrients.

The vast majority of fruits and vegetables can be eaten in their raw, natural state, including less obvious choices such as rhubarb, sweet potato, aubergine (eggplant) and cauliflower. Fresh fruits and veggies are the mainstay of a balanced and healthy raw food diet.

Green Vitality

Raw foodist Victoria Boutenko and her family healed themselves of various chronic illnesses by embracing a raw food diet. They ate mostly fresh fruit, nuts and seeds. After a period of life-changing improvement, their sense of wellbeing started to decline. Victoria decided to study the diet of our closest relative, the chimpanzee, and discovered that they ate a surprisingly large number of green leaves as part of their daily diet. Victoria and her family started consuming daily green smoothies as part of their wellness regime. Their health improved dramatically and daily fresh greens have become an essential part of the ultimately healthy diet ever since.

Sprouted Seeds & Legumes

Sprouted seeds and legumes are little superfood miracles. Considering their size they pack an amazing nutritional punch. The amount of energy and nutrients that a plant contains when it first starts to grow (sprout) is proportionally huge.

Sprouted seeds and legumes are an incredibly good source of protein as well as many other essential nutrients, including essential fatty acids needed for the health of every cell in your body. You can grow your own sprouts (*see* page 80) or buy them from a good health food store.

Fresh Herbs & Spices

Fresh herbs and spices take raw food to a new level of sophistication. Favourite fresh spices include chillies, ginger, kaffir lime leaves and lemongrass. The most useful fresh herbs tend to be basil, coriander (cilantro), rosemary and chives. Use them to jazz up salads, raw pasta dishes and raw crackers.

THE STORECUPBOARD

While fresh produce makes up the bulk of a raw food diet, you will want to stock your cupboards with deliciously nutritious dried ingredients too. These ingredients will be used in everything from breakfasts to main meals to desserts.

Nuts & Seeds

Nuts and seeds are one of the major sources of protein in a raw food diet. They are also a fantastic source of essential healthy fats, as well as vitamin E. Nuts and seeds are used as the base ingredients in raw pâtés, cakes, tarts and cheeses as well as a nutritionally important addition to breakfasts, salads and sweet treats.

Clockwise from top left: sprouted lentils, ginger, nut and coriander pâté, hulled hemp seeds

Dried Herbs & Spices

Keeping a selection of dried herbs and spices will mean that you can make more exciting raw recipes. Favourite dried herbs include oregano, tarragon and Italian mixed herbs. Spices that will serve you well include ready-mixed curry powder, ground cumin, ground coriander and whole black peppercorns for grinding.

Salt is essential to health. There are 'good' and 'bad' sources of salt, so it is important to use only unprocessed sea salts and rock salts, such as Himalayan pink salt. Avoid sea salt that has been processed, as its full-spectrum minerals have been removed.

Superfoods

Superfoods are an incredibly powerful way to significantly boost the quantity of high-quality nutrients in your diet. Most superfoods are very potent and you only need small amounts of them to experience the benefits.

SPIRULINA & CHLORELLA

These are green algae, which you can buy in powdered form. They are one of the best sources of super-healthy essential fatty acids, as well as being high in protein and iron. Add them to smoothies.

SEAWEED

This is a fantastic source of protein and the mineral iodine. Iodine is essential for hormone regulation. If you are taking medication for a thyroid condition, it is best to consult your doctor about the impact of eating seaweed alongside your medication before making it part of your regular diet. Add it to salads and Asian-inspired main meals.

BEE POLLEN

This is the pollen harvested by bees. Although it is not a vegan product, sprinkling bee pollen on your breakfast, desserts and smoothies will give you a good supply

Clockwise from top: goji berries, spirulina powder, cacao, amaranth seeds, bee pollen, cape gooseberries

of B vitamins, including B12, without eating animal products. Sprinkle bee pollen on breakfasts, and add it to raw sweet treats and smoothies.

MACA

This is a powder made from the dried root of a plant from the horseradish family. It grows high in the mountains and has been used in Chinese medicine and traditional healing cultures for thousands of years. Maca is believed to be an adaptogenic hormone balancer and has been used to treat health issues linked to menstruation, menopause and depression. If you are on HRT (hormone replacement therapy), please consult your doctor before introducing maca into your diet. Add to smoothies.

CACAO

The raw form of the chocolate bean, cacao comes in the form of whole beans, chopped beans (cacao nibs) or the ground bean, which is separated into its component parts of fibre (cacao powder,) and fat (cacao butter). Cacao is a fantastic source of minerals,

Above left: maca powder and root; Above: cacao beans and powder

including magnesium, and protein. It also contains a small amount of caffeine, which can be very stimulating. Use raw cacao in smoothies and desserts.

CHIA & FLAXSEEDS

These are both high in essential fatty acids (EFAs) and other essential nutrients. These simple seeds are far more nutritionally powerful than they look and are a great addition to your daily diet. They will help to keep your mood and weight balanced and your body hydrated. EFAs are integral to maintaining the hydration, and therefore health, of your body's cells. Add chia and flaxseeds to breakfasts, smoothies and sweet treats.

Oils

Oils, and fat in general, have had a bad rap over the years due to an incomplete understanding of their function. The standard diet contains many sources of unhealthy fat that contributes to weight gain and heart disease. However, fat per se is not the issue. Healthy fats are essential to our wellbeing.

Above: chia pudding; Above right: chia seeds

They are one of the major building blocks used to form and repair our cells. A lack of healthy fat can also contribute to a lack of good health.

The most frequently used healthy sources of fat in a raw food diet include extra virgin coconut oil, olive oil and hemp oil. Other healthful and tasty oils include walnut oil, avocado oil and flax oil.

Raw oils are labelled cold-pressed and extra virgin. It is important to buy your oils raw, as the process of heat treating oils destroys their healthy structure and turns them into 'bad' fats.

Vinegars

Unpasteurized vinegars are the only true raw vinegars. However, a little balsamic, wine or rice vinegar can add an interesting flavour dimension to a dressing or sauce without detracting from the major health benefits of a raw dish. Unpasteurized apple cider vinegar is the most easily found raw vinegar.

Sweeteners

There is a lot of controversy around raw sweeteners, particularly agave syrup. Some people believe that they are not as healthy as they have claimed.

While it is true that the healthiest sweet foods you can eat are whole, unprocessed fruits, raw sweeteners such as agave, yacon and unpasteurized honey are very good sources of minerals and carbohydrates.

Weaning yourself off sugar is one of the most healthful practices you can embrace. If you want to kick a refined sugar addiction then raw sweeteners can be a good bridge. They are less addictive than refined sugar and therefore easier to reduce in the long run.

The healthiest of all sweeteners is stevia. Stevia does not contain any form of sugar, but instead acts to open up the taste buds that detect sweetness. In this way, it naturally enhances the sweetness present in the food already. Stevia is brilliant for diabetics or anyone who cannot process a lot of fruit sugar or raw sweetness.

Other sweeteners are becoming more common, such as coconut and palm sugar. Again, these contain healthy nutrients but should be used with consideration. Adding sweetness to your meals should be limited to occasional treats rather than used regularly.

Grains

Many grains can be sprouted and eaten in their raw form. They are used in raw crackers, salads and main meals. Ancient wheat grains, such as spelt, are much easier to digest in their sprouted form. The gluten is broken down in the sprouting process and those with gluten intolerances often find they can eat sprouted wheat grains in this way.

Other grains, which are delicious in their raw, sprouted form include quinoa, millet, amaranth and barley. Rice does not sprout and therefore cannot be eaten raw. However, some people enjoy sprouted wild rice, which is, strictly speaking, not actually from the rice family and can be eaten raw.

A NOTE ON OATS:

Oats in their whole and rolled forms are not raw. As a general practice, oats are steam-treated on harvest and lose their raw status at this point, but they are still a great source of healthy fibre and other nutrients and are often used in raw recipes. You may be able to buy fresh, whole raw oats online or from specialist health shops, but they must be treated as fresh produce rather than as a dry grain, as they spoil in the same way fresh vegetables do.

FROZEN FOODS

If you have a busy life or like to be efficient, it is possible to freeze raw foods. Freezing is a great way to be prepared and is especially useful when it comes to having a stock of frozen nut or seed milks as well as desserts.

Freezing is a great way to preserve a glut of ripe bananas and avocados, as well as fresh berries, for direct use in smoothies and raw ice creams.

Prepackaged frozen fruits and vegetables from the frozen section of the supermarket have usually been cooked or pasteurized before packaging and are not considered raw.

FOODS TO AVOID

Foods that should not be eaten raw in any form include standard white potatoes, rice (apart from wild rice) and kidney beans.

Prepackaged milks, including almond and coconut milks, and the majority of prepacked juices have been pasteurized and so are not considered raw.

It is best not to eat fresh, water-rich fruits at the same time as nuts and seeds. Fresh fruit is digested very quickly, while nuts and seeds take longer. When both are in your stomach at the same time, the fruit ferments while the nuts are taking longer to digest, often causing discomfort and bloating.

SHOPPING TIPS

Raw food shopping can seem a little daunting at first, but you will soon get used to having large quantities of vibrantly fresh and colourful produce in your shopping trolley.

Most of your weekly shop will take place in the fruit and vegetable aisles of the supermarket, your local grocery store or farmers' markets.

Supplementary shopping trips to your local health food store, or an online health food emporium, will also be part of stocking up for your healthy eating lifestyle.

Bulk buying your cupboard ingredients can save costs as well as being more convenient. This can be done online or through local food co-operatives.

Depending on the content of your previous diet, eating more raw food may or may not be a more expensive lifestyle choice.

If you are deciding to eat more raw and significantly less meat, fish, cheese, ready-prepared meals, wine and prepackaged drinks and snacks then you will find that a raw food lifestyle may in fact be cheaper. If you are used to eating a basic vegetarian or vegan wholefood diet, you will probably need to invest a bit more in order to increase the amount of life-enhancing raw foods in your diet.

TOOLS & EQUIPMENT

BASIC KIT

Easy raw food recipes simply need a knife, a chopping board and a basic blender. Fancy equipment is not necessary to get started with raw food, but if you want to get more creative with your recipes, you may want to add extra kitchen tools to your range as you go.

Slicing & Dicing

Sharp knives will become your best friends when preparing raw food. Most raw recipes call for some kind of slicing, dicing and chopping, so having sharp knives will reduce preparation time.

There are many knife-sharpening options on the market, from easy-to-use pull-through sharpeners to pro-chef sharpening tools. Choose a style that suits your knife-sharpening proficiency.

Blending

Many raw food recipes call for a blender, to create creamy and smooth textured foods, such as smoothies and sauces. A wand or stick blender is a great way to get started with raw food. Jug blenders are also very useful if you want to prepare food for more than one.

Processing

A food processor is used to quickly chop fruit, vegetables, nuts and other ingredients. If you do not have much space then, rather than a specialized food processor, choose

a wand blender that comes with a food processing attachment in the form of a separate bowl with a chopping blade and lid.

Juicing

Juicing is extracting the fresh juice from raw fruits and vegetables. Drinking freshly made juice is one of the quickest ways to enhance your health and sense of wellbeing. Fresh juices are packed with vitamins, minerals, electrolytes and phytonutrients and a mixed greens and fruit juice is the most health-restoring multivitamin available.

Juicing machines, also known as juicers, come in a selection of mechanical styles. Choosing which juicer to buy will depend on your lifestyle, budget and ultimate health aims.

CENTRIFUGAL JUICERS

These are at the budget end of the juicer scale. They are quick to use and relatively easy to clean, taking 10–15 minutes to make a large glass of juice and clean the machine. The easiest centrifugal juicers have large chutes so that you can put your fruit and vegetables in whole rather than having to chop it up first. The downside of centrifugal juicers is that the process they use to extract juice – grating and spinning – destroys more of the fragile nutrients than auger juicers. This said, a centrifugal juicer will suit you best if you are short on time and are prepared to forgo nutrients for speed and ease.

AUGER JUICERS

These are the crème de la crème of juicers. There are two types of auger juicer: single auger and twin auger. The auger is the part of the juicer that slowly spins and crushes the fruits and vegetables to press out their juice. Although these juicers take longer to extract juice and clean – 20–25 minutes to make a large glass of juice and clean the machine – the quality of the juice is superior in taste and nutrient content to centrifugal juicers. An auger juicer will suit you if you are aiming for the best health possible and are prepared to be patient while you juice.

Grinding

Grinding is the process of making fine powders or flours from dried ingredients. Raw foods that often need to be ground for specific recipes include nuts and seeds, spices, dried coconut and grains such as buckwheat. Raw flours are used in desserts, raw pastry cases (shells) and dehydrated crackers.

Grinding can be done by hand in small quantities using a pestle and mortar. A more efficient way to create powdered or floured ingredients is to use a coffee or spice grinder, or the grinding attachment that comes with some food processors.

Straining

In the raw food kitchen, straining is used to make nut and seed milks as well as to drain excess juice or liquid from prepared ingredients.

A nut milk bag or large square of muslin cloth (cheesecloth) is useful
for preparing raw milks and, if you do not have a juicer, fresh juices.
It is also possible to use a clean dish towel or other clean fabric for
straining. The thinner the straining fabric, the easier it will be to strain the
liquid through it.

For other types of straining, a colander as well as a large and small sieve
(strainer) will also serve you well.

Purifying

Water is an essential part of a healthy diet. Most water from the tap contains
chlorine, fluoride and other potentially harmful chemicals, as well as hormones
from the contraceptive pill and other medication residues that are not filtered
out during the recycling process. For this reason, it is advisable to filter tap
water in some way before using it.

Some people like to install in-house filtration systems for all their water, including bathing water. More simply, using a filter jug for your drinking and cooking water will mean that you are ingesting fewer harmful substances and increasing the quality of your water.

THE NEXT LEVEL

If you enjoy making beautiful plates of food and love getting creative in the kitchen then it is likely you will want to invest in some extra equipment. You may already have a lot of great kitchen tools, waiting to be used in a new capacity to make raw food recipes, and a lot of standard kitchen equipment can easily be repurposed.

You may also want to upgrade your equipment in order to reduce the amount of time you spend in the kitchen. Bigger, faster, diverse kitchen tools will speed up food prep time so you can increase your raw energy with super-efficiency.

Slicing, Dicing & Spiralising

Taking your slicing and dicing to the next level can be really fun and creative. There are a number of gadgets and kitchen implements that will allow you to do paper-thin slices, quick juliennes (matchstick sized strips), zesting, super-quick grating and dicing and spaghetti-like vegetable noodles.

A mandolin is a lovely piece of kitchen kit that is especially good for making more gourmet recipes. With a mandolin, you can create uniform slices, including paper-thin slices that are hard to achieve using a knife.

You have probably seen courgettes (zucchini) and carrots prepared to look like spaghetti or noodles. Vegetables prepared in this way are a favourite with raw foodies. It is quick and easy to prepare as a low-carb, gluten-free alternative to traditional pasta and noodles. To make your own raw spaghetti you will need a simple piece of equipment called a spiralizer. Spiralizers come in different styles – some are small enough to fit into a drawer, like the GEFU, while others, such as the Lurch Spiralizer, will require cupboard or worktop space.

A julienne peeler is a simple peeler-style piece of kitchen equipment that cuts fruits and vegetables into fine, matchstick-like strips. A julienne peeler is a great way of introducing a different texture to salads and main meals.

A zester helps you to remove the sweet, flavoursome zest from citrus fruits without including the bitter pith underneath. Lemon and orange zests are used to give an exotic or summery twist to salad dressings, main meals and raw dessert recipes.

The slicing disc and blade attachments that come with food processors are very useful for super-quick chopping and grating. They are particularly good for making large quantities of sliced, diced and grated fruits and vegetables for when you are entertaining or making bulk batches.

Blending

High-speed blenders are a serious raw food enthusiast's best friend. Used for blending and grinding, they make light work of many everyday recipes. For speed and efficiency, they cannot be beaten.

High-speed blenders, such as those from Vitamix and Blendtec, can blend whole fruits and vegetables in a matter of seconds. At the touch of a button, in under 5 minutes, you can have smoothies, soups, sauces, dressings and desserts on the table and ready to eat.

Although they are a luxury purchase, a high-speed blender is one of the best investments you can make in your long-term health and wellbeing. Being able to make delicious raw food recipes more quickly than cooked ones will make the difference between reaching for a slice of toast and whizzing up a nutritious smoothie instead.

Processing

A good-quality high-speed food processor usually comes with discs and blades for mixing, processing, slicing, dicing and grating. Investing in a high-speed food processor such as one by Cuisinart or KitchenAid will decrease raw food preparation time. High-speed food processors are particularly good for making batch recipes to freeze or store, or if you are making food for lots of people.

Sprouting

As we have seen, sprouting is the name given to growing seeds into young plant shoots for use as a raw food, turning them into nutritional powerhouses. The easiest way to grown your own sprouts is to use simple but specially designed sprouting jars or sprouting trays. See page 80 for more information on sprouting.

Dehydrating

Dehydrating is how the raw food world describes raw foods that have been dried at temperatures below 45°C/113°F. You can use a dehydrator to make raw crackers, crisps (chips) and dried fruit as well as to warm or partially dry out raw burgers, quiches and other recipes.

Dehydrating is usually done using a dehydrating machine. If you live in a warm climate, it is possible to sun-dry raw foods. It is also possible to dehydrate raw foods if you have an oven or range that has a very low temperature setting.

A dehydrator consists of a box with mesh shelves and a warm fan to dry out the raw ingredients. Many recipes that involve dehydrating begin as a wet mixture, so it is important to have specialized nonstick dehydrating sheets for these wetter recipes. Most dehydrators either come with these specialist sheets, or you can buy them as extras.

PREPARATION & TECHNIQUES

FOOD SAFETY & HYGIENE

Raw and fresh fruits and vegetables need to be rinsed well before using. Food poisoning from raw food is very rare as it generally contains no animal products, the main culprit in food poisoning. It is, however, possible to get a mildly upset stomach from the bacteria on unwashed fruits and vegetables. If you have animal products in your refrigerator, keep them contained on a separate shelf to your raw food ingredients. It is a good idea to have separate chopping (cutting) boards for fruit, vegetables, fish and meat to avoid cross-contamination.

HOW TO:

Raw food preparation is mostly simple, but there are tips and tricks that make recipes even more easy and fun to make.

Cut

Although it may seem obvious, dicing and chopping are necessary simple skills for almost all raw food recipes. There is different terminology for various types of cut ingredients, from finely chopped to bite-size. But what do they mean?

Dice/chop – cut into rough pieces about 0.5–1 cm/¼–½ inch in size
Finely dice/chop – cut into pieces about 1–3 mm/¹⁄₁₆–⅛ inch in size
Chop into bite-size pieces – cut into about 2.5 cm/1 inch cubes
Slice – cut into slices about 0.5–1 cm/¼–½ inch wide
Finely slice – cut into slices about 1–3 mm/¹⁄₁₆–⅛ inch wide

Blend

To make blending with a hand blender easier, and to give a smoother final texture, cut or grate your ingredients into small pieces. The softer the fruit or vegetables, the larger your pieces can be. So, for example, grate harder ingredients like carrots, parsnips and apples before blending, and cut softer ingredients like bananas, tomatoes and avocadoes into larger bite-size pieces.

When you are making a raw recipe in a high-speed blender, there is no need to chop your ingredients first. Put the soft water-based ingredients into the jug and the drier ingredients in last.

Strain

Making your own nut and seed milks is much easier than you would imagine. They are a deliciously creamy, healthy alternative to dairy milks and prepackaged dairy alternatives.

To make raw milks, first blend your soaked and rinsed nuts and/or seeds with the specified amount of water.

Place your nut milk bag or straining cloth in a bowl or jug (pitcher) large enough to contain your blended mixture.

Pour the mixture into the straining cloth and bowl. Holding the top edges of the cloth, lift it above the bowl. Squeeze the bag until you have squeezed out as much of the liquid as you can.

Juice

Juicing is actually an easy four-step process:

1 Wash your juicing ingredients.

2 Cut your fruit and vegetables into pieces that will fit down the chute of your juicer.

3 Juice your ingredients.

4 Pour out the juice and wash your juicer.

To make juicing quicker, chop all your ingredients up ready for juicing before you start. To make cleaning your juicer easy, wash it up as soon as you have finished juicing. Some juicers create a pulpy juice. If you prefer a smoother juice, strain it before drinking. For optimum nutrition, freshly made juice should be drunk within 15 minutes of making.

Sprout

The first step in sprouting is to soak your seeds overnight. This releases the enzyme inhibitors, the natural chemicals that keep seeds in their dormant state, and provides nutrients for the seed to absorb for its initial growth.

Next, rinse your seeds 2–3 times in clean water. Drain the seeds and put them in your sprouting jars or trays.

Water and drain your seeds 2–3 times a day until they reach their optimum sprout size.

Depending on the type of seeds you are sprouting, it takes between 1–7 days to grow sprouts. For specific sprouting times, please refer to a specialist sprouting book or look online.

Dehydrate

There are different kinds of foods to have fun dehydrating. Firstly, there are whole foods, such as dried apples, mangos and tomatoes. Secondly, there are raw recipes such as raw crackers, fruit leathers and vegetable chips.

To dehydrate larger fruits, such as apples, bananas and mangos, cut them into slices, about 3–5 mm/⅛–¼ inch thick. To dehydrate smaller fruit, such as grapes, strawberries or apricots, cut them into halves or quarters. To dehydrate tomatoes, cut them into halves or slices. Dehydrate for 12–24 hours, until all the water has evaporated.

For recipes that involve dehydration to produce, for example, crackers and fruit leathers, place the mixture on the dehydrator's greaseproof (wax) sheets. Spread the mixture

evenly with a spatula or large, flat knife to the specified thickness. If the recipe calls for it, score your flattened mixture with the back of a knife. When the mixture has dried out, these scored lines will be easy to break into even-sized pieces. For this kind of recipe, dehydration usually takes 18–24 hours.

If your ingredients are fully dehydrated, they will keep for up to a month in an airtight container. If your ingredients are not fully dehydrated, keep them in the refrigerator and eat them within a few days, otherwise they will become mouldy.

Spiralize

Raw spaghetti – also known as courgetti because it is most often made with raw courgette (zucchini) – can actually be made with any firm vegetable.

The best vegetables to use with a spiralizer include courgettes (zucchini), as mentioned, carrots, beetroot (beets) and squash. These vegetables are firm enough to maintain the spaghetti shape created by the spiralizer.

Courgette (zucchini) is most commonly used to make raw spaghetti because it has a neutral flavour and does not dye a recipe with its juice, as beetroot (beets) and carrots do.

To spiralize courgettes (zucchini), simply rinse and cut them in half, so you have 2 shorter lengths. Place the flat cut end of the courgette (zucchini) onto the cutting blades of your spiralizer and the stalk end onto the spinning point of the spiralizer handle. With the handle, push the courgette (zucchini) onto the blades while turning the handle at the same time to create raw spaghetti. If the blades cut half-moon shapes instead of long strings, try turning the handle in the opposite direction.

Spiralising creates very long strings of vegetables. To make them more manageable to eat, cut your pile of courgetti across the middle with a knife, before adding the rest of the ingredients and serving.

Soak & Rehydrate

Dried nuts, seeds, fruits and vegetables benefit from soaking and rehydrating.

It is particularly important to soak dried seeds and brown-skinned nuts. Dried nuts and seeds, while still good for you prior to soaking, release their enzyme inhibitors and improve their nutritional content when soaked.

To soak nuts and seeds, place the desired quantity of dried nuts or seeds in a bowl with 2–3 times the amount of water. Allow seeds to rehydrate for at least 4 hours, and nuts for at least 8 hours. Drain and discard the soaking water before rinsing them in clean water.

If you are not going to use your soaked nuts, seeds or fruits, store them in an airtight container in the refrigerator and use them within 3 days.

Nuts without brown skins, such as cashew nuts, pine nuts and macadamia nuts, do not need to be soaked unless you wish to soften them for a recipe.

To rehydrate dried fruits and vegetables such as sun-dried tomatoes, dried mushrooms, raisins and prunes, place them in a bowl with twice as much water. Allow to rehydrate for at least 60 minutes. The flavoursome soaking water can be added to smoothies, soups, sauces and dressings.

STAPLE RECIPES

ALMOND MILK

Almond milk is a delicious alternative to dairy milk. Home-made almond milk is far superior in nutritional content and taste to ready-made brands available in the shops.

Makes 400 ml/ 14 fl oz/ 1²/₃ cups

200 g/7 oz/1¼ cups soaked raw almonds
450 ml/¾ pint/1¾ cups water

Soak the almonds for at least 8 hours, or overnight.

After soaking, rinse the nuts, then put into a high-speed blender with the water and blend the water until smooth and creamy.

Strain the mixture using a nut milk bag or cloth. Alternatively, use the almond milk without straining out the pulp.

Store fresh almond milk in the refrigerator for up to 24 hours or freeze for up to 2 weeks.

SWEET CASHEW MILK

This sweet, creamy milk does not require straining, so it is quick and easy to make. It works particularly well in smoothies and desserts.

Makes 200 ml/7 fl oz/¾ cup

200 ml/7 fl oz/¾ cup water
1 date, pitted
pinch mineral salt
50 g/2 oz/⅓ cup cashew nuts

Blend all the ingredients together until smooth and creamy. The milk is ready to serve or use in a recipe.

Chill in the refrigerator for up to 24 hours or freeze it for up to 2 weeks.

Note

If you are using a stick blender, soften the cashews by soaking them in water for at least 4 hours, or overnight. Discard the soaking water.

CASHEW NUT CHEESE

Cashew nut cheese is delicious and satisfying as an alternative to dairy cheese. Eat it on crackers or wheat-free toast, and top raw pasta dishes with it too.

Makes 1 cheese round

300g/11 oz/2 cups cashew nuts

2 tbsp water

2 tbsp lime juice

1 garlic clove

15 g/½ oz/¼ cup nutritional yeast flakes

1 tsp mineral salt

chilli flakes, for sprinkling (optional)

Soak the cashews in water for 2–4 hours, then drain.

Place the cashews in a blender or food processor with the water, lime juice, garlic, yeast flakes and salt and blend until smooth and creamy. Turn out onto a flat work surface and shape it into a circular cheese round using a spatula.

Alternatively, line a bowl with clingfilm (plastic wrap) and press the mixture into the bowl. Tip the bowl upside down onto a serving plate or board and remove the clingfilm (plastic wrap).

Sprinkle the cheese round with chilli flakes, if using, and leave to set in the refrigerator for 1–2 hours.

Serve with raw crackers or gluten-free wholegrain toast. Eat fresh or freeze for up to a month.

ALMOND BUTTER

The fragile and healthy oils in almonds are still fresh and nutritious in this home-made butter. Fresh almond butter works brilliantly as a simple spread, as well as to enrich raw smoothies and soups.

Makes one 250 g/9 oz container

250 g/9 oz/2⅔ cups ground raw almonds
2 tbsp cold-pressed hemp oil
large pinch mineral salt (optional)

Grind the almonds in a spice grinder or high-speed blender until fine for smooth butter or coarse for crunchy butter. Stir in the hemp oil and salt, if using, until it is evenly distributed.

Decant the butter into an airtight container or jar and store in the refrigerator. Eat within 1 week, or store in the freezer for up to a month.

SESAME & SUNFLOWER CRISPBREAD

This satisfying crispbread is full of healthy omega oils to help increase brain function, balance mood and keep joints lubricated. Use them as an alternative to bread and gluten-based crackers.

Makes 2 dehydrator trays of crispbreads

65 g/2½ oz/½ cup brown flaxseeds
80 g/3 oz/½ cup ground brown flaxseeds
80 g/3 oz/½ cup sesame seeds
70 g/2½ oz/½ cup sunflower seeds
225 g/8 oz/2 cups grated sweet potato
juice of 1 lemon
80 g/3 oz/½ cup onion, peeled and chopped
½ tsp mineral salt

Mix all the ingredients together thoroughly in a food processor. If the mixture is too dry for it to turn easily in the processor bowl, add 1 tablespoon of water at a time until the mixture is turning easily.

Put 2 dehydrator greaseproof (wax) sheets onto 2 dehydrator trays. Using a rubber spatula, divide the mixture in half and spread it flat onto the sheets.

Score the flattened mixture into the size you would like your crispbreads to be, then dehydrate at 45°C/113°F for about 8 hours.

Remove the partially dehydrated crispbreads from the dehydrator sheets and place the crackers back onto the mesh shelves of your dehydrator. Dehydrate for a further 8–12 hours until totally crisp and dry. Store the crackers in an airtight container for up to a month.

FLAXSEED & TOMATO CRACKERS

Deliciously crunchy, these healthy crackers work equally well as an accompaniment to dips and as a bread substitute. The sun-dried tomatoes give them a lovely richness and depth of flavour.

Makes 3 dehydrator trays of crackers

150 g/5 oz/generous 1 cup flaxseeds

75 g/3 oz/1⅓ cups dry sun-dried tomatoes (not in oil)

500 ml/18 fl oz/2 cups water

5 tomatoes

juice of ½ lemon

1 garlic clove, peeled

½ tsp tamari

Soak the flaxseeds and sun-dried tomatoes in the water for at least 8 hours, or overnight.

Blend together all the ingredients, including the soaking water, in a food processor. Divide the mixture into 3 roughly equal portions. Place each portion onto a dehydrator tray lined with a dehydrator greaseproof (wax) sheet, spreading the mixture flat with a spatula.

Dehydrate at 45°C/113°C for 4–6 hours.

Remove the partially dehydrated crackers from the dehydrator sheets, then using scissors, cut each large square into small squares or triangles to use with dips, or into larger squares to use instead of bread in sandwiches.

Place the crackers back onto the mesh shelves of your dehydrator and dehydrate for a further 14 hours, until thoroughly crisp and dry.

When fully dehydrated, these crackers will last for up to a month or so in an airtight container.

BREAKFAST

QUINOA, FRUIT & NUT BOWL

Quinoa is rich in protein, so eating it for breakfast is a great start to the day. This recipe combines the freshness of a fruit salad with the long-lasting energy boost of nuts and superfood quinoa sprouts.

Makes 1 bowl

8 raw whole almonds
40 g/1½ oz/¼ cup raw red, white or black whole quinoa grains, sprouted
75 g/3 oz/½ cup mixed fruit, such as mixed berries, mango, kiwi fruit and raisins

Soak the almonds in water overnight, then drain and rinse.

Place the sprouted quinoa in a bowl and top with fresh fruit and the soaked almonds.

Your breakfast is now ready to eat or to put in an airtight container to take to work.

Note

Quinoa takes 2 days to sprout. Soak the raw quinoa overnight, then the next day, drain and rinse in the morning, afternoon and evening. The following morning, drain and rinse one final time, then they are ready to use.

BERRY SMOOTHIE BOWL

This delicious smoothie bowl is packed full of antioxidants and vitamin C to boost your immune system. Eat it early or take it to work as a late breakfast or mid-morning snack.

Makes 1 bowl

2 large handfuls raspberries
2 large handfuls blueberries or blackberries
1 ripe banana, peeled
150 ml/¼ pint/⅔ cup water

For the topping
small handful goji berries
small handful sunflower seeds
small handful pumpkin seeds
small handful chia seeds

Blend the raspberries, blueberries/blackberries, banana and water.

Decant the berry smoothie into a bowl and top with the goji berries, sunflower seeds, pumpkin seeds and chia seeds before diving in.

BIRCHER MUESLI

Bircher muesli is a traditional breakfast that is long-lasting and satisfying. It is particularly good when you are in need of a comforting breakfast at the weekend or on cold, rainy days.

Makes 1 bowl

50 g/2 oz/½ cup rolled oats
handful raisins
200 ml/7 fl oz/¾ cup water or raw nut or seed milk
handful raw whole almonds
1 apple, grated (with skin on, if liked)
raw agave syrup or raw honey to sweeten (optional)

The evening before, combine the rolled oats, raisins and water or nut milk in a breakfast bowl. In a separate bowl, soak the almonds in water.

The next morning, drain and rinse the almonds, then chop them up. Add them to the oat mixture with the grated apple. Sweeten with agave syrup or honey, if using, and enjoy.

CHIA PUDDING WITH FRUIT

When chia seeds are combined with nut milk, they create a creamy, textured breakfast that is both satisfyingly rich and healthy. Without the fresh fruit, this recipe will keep in the refrigerator for 3 days.

Makes 1 bowl

200 ml/7 fl oz/¾ cup fresh raw almond milk (*see* page 88)

1 tbsp + 1 tsp raw agave syrup or raw honey

¼ tsp vanilla extract

3 tbsp chia seeds

75 g/3 oz/½ cup blueberries

½ banana, peeled and sliced

10 seedless white grapes

The evening before, combine the almond milk, 1 tablespoon of the agave syrup or honey, the vanilla extract and chia seeds in a bowl. Stir regularly for the first 30 minutes of soaking, to avoid clumping. Cover and chill in the refrigerator overnight.

The next morning, blend half of the blueberries with 1 teaspoon of agave syrup or honey in a blender, then pour the berry purée on top of the chia mixture. Top with rest the remaining blueberries, slices of banana and grapes and enjoy.

JUICES & SMOOTHIES

SPINACH & KIWI SMOOTHIE

Raw green veggies are the best way to get some of the most essential vitamins and minerals into your diet. This easy smoothie works well as a breakfast or as a quick afternoon snack.

Makes 1 large glass or 2 smaller glasses

freshly squeezed juice of 2 oranges

6 ice cubes

3 kiwi fruits, peeled

75 g/3 oz/2½ cups spinach

1 banana, peeled

Blend all the ingredients together in a blender until smooth.

Pour into a glass and drink immediately for ultimate nutritional value.

KALE & APPLE SMOOTHIE

Kale and apple is a classic raw food combination. If your blender is not very powerful, shred the kale into small pieces and remove any stalks before starting.

Makes 1 large glass or 2 smaller glasses

50 g/2 oz kale

2 apples, cored

2 Medjool dates, pitted

juice of ½ lemon

300 ml/½ pint/1¼ cups water

Remove any tough stalks from the kale, then add to a blender with the remaining ingredients and blend together until smooth.

Pour into a tall glass and serve.

BEETROOT & APPLE JUICE

The colour of this refreshing juice is beautiful. Enjoy drinking in the jewelled colour, knowing that you are boosting your immune system and cleansing your blood at the same time.

Makes 1 large glass or 2 smaller glasses

1 beetroot (beet)

4 apples

½ lemon, with peel

1 cm/½ inch piece fresh ginger, peeled

Cut the beetroot (beet), apples and lemon into pieces that will fit into the juicer chute.

Juice the beetroot (beet), apples, lemon and ginger together.

Pour into a glass and serve immediately for maximum nutritional benefit.

ALMOND, LEMON & GINGER SMOOTHIE

This smoothie is a real treat. Based on a Spanish bitter lemon drink, which uses whole lemons, the sweet creaminess of the almond and dates balances the alkalising tartness of the lemon and ginger.

Makes 1 medium glass

½ lemon

300 ml/½ pint/1¼ cups fresh raw almond milk (*see* page 88)

1 cm/½ inch piece fresh ginger, peeled

6 Medjool dates, pitted

Zest the lemon with a fine grater or citrus zester (only zest the yellow skin, as the white pith underneath is bitter).

Juice the lemon and add the juice to the blender with the lemon zest, almond milk, ginger and pitted dates.

Blend all the ingredients together in a blender until smooth and creamy.

If you are not using a high-speed blender, strain the mixture through a muslin cloth (cheesecloth) or nut milk bag to remove the pulp before serving.

Pour into a glass and drink immediately.

BEETROOT & BERRY SMOOTHIE

Berries are high in vitamin C and antioxidants and beetroot is known for its blood-cleansing qualities, so this smoothie not only tastes great, it is also wonderful for detoxing.

Makes 1 large glass or 2 smaller glasses

½ beetroot (beet), peeled

75 g/3 oz/½ cup blueberries

75 g/3 oz/scant ⅔ cup raspberries

75 g/3 oz/½ cup strawberries

1 banana, peeled

200 ml/7 fl oz/¾ cup water

4 ice cubes

Blend all the ingredients together in a blender until smooth and creamy.

Pour into a tall glass and serve immediately.

Note

If you are using a less powerful blender, grate the beetroot (beet) first.

CARROT & APPLE JUICE

This recipe is a classic, which is often found in juice and smoothie bars all over the world. However, it is never better than when you make it at home, especially if you use organic ingredients.

Makes 1 medium glass

5 carrots
2 apples
¼ lemon, with peel

Cut the carrots, apples and lemon into pieces that will fit into the juicer chute.

Juice the carrots, apples and lemon together.

Pour into a glass and serve immediately for maximum nutritional benefit.

STRAWBERRY MILKSHAKE

This milkshake is the taste of summer in a glass. Kids and adults love it as a healthy alternative to dairy-based milkshakes. Serve it as it is or topped with a few fresh strawberries.

Makes 1 large glass or 2 smaller glasses

200 g/7 oz/1⅓ cups strawberries, hulled

2 Medjool dates, pitted

300 ml/½ pint/1¼ cups fresh raw almond milk (*see* page 88)

6 ice cubes

Blend all the ingredients together in a blender until smooth and creamy.

Pour into a tall glass and serve immediately.

YELLOW SMOOTHIE

This filling fruity smoothie will get your taste buds dancing as a slimming breakfast, as light lunch or as a quick healthy snack.

Makes 1 large glass or 2 smaller glasses

150 ml/5 fl oz/⅔ cup water

1 small ripe mango, peeled and stoned

100 g/3½ oz ripe pineapple, peeled and cored

juice of ½ lemon

4 ice cubes

1 banana, peeled

½ apple, peeled and cored

Blend all the ingredients together in a blender until smooth and creamy.

Pour into a tall glass and serve immediately.

DIPS, SAUCES & SNACKS

COURGETTE & CARROT ROLLS

These gorgeous rolls can be made and immediately popped into your mouth, or pinned with toothpicks and plated up beautifully as an appetizer. They are super fresh and demonstrate all that is good about raw food.

Makes about 10

For the rolls

1 large carrot, peeled

1 large courgette (zucchini)

1 red (bell) pepper

1 quantity cashew mayonnaise (*see* page 146)

handful fresh leafy herb sprigs or pea sprouts

For the dipping sauce

2 tbsp gluten-free soy sauce or tamari

1 tbsp raw honey or raw agave syrup

1 garlic clove, peeled and crushed

½ large red chilli, seeded and finely diced

Mix all the dipping sauce ingredients together in a bowl and set aside.

Using a mandolin or sharp knife, cut the carrot and courgette (zucchini) into long slices, about 3 mm/⅛ inch thick, then cut the red (bell) pepper into long matchsticks.

Spoon 1 teaspoon of cashew mayonnaise onto the larger end of each carrot slice. Position 6–8 red (bell) pepper matchsticks on top of the mayonnaise and add a sprig of fresh herb or pea sprouts.

Gently roll the carrot slices up, then with half a toothpick, at an angle, carefully pin the rolls closed with the sharp end.

Repeat with the courgette (zucchini) slices, using 2 teaspoon cashew mayonnaise instead.

Serve with the dipping sauce.

NUT-FILLED MUSHROOMS

The nuttiness of walnuts and chestnut (cremini) mushrooms make a wonderful marriage of flavours. These sophisticated little bites are perfect as part of a canapé selection or as a starter (appetizer) for a dinner party.

Makes 8

50 g/1¾ oz/½ cup walnuts

8 chestnut (cremini) mushrooms

2 tbsp extra virgin olive oil

juice of ½ lime

2 tbsp water

1 chopped whole spring onion (scallion)

¼ tsp mineral salt

½ tsp smoked paprika

1 tbsp vegan pesto (*see* page 149)

Soak the walnuts in water for at least 8 hours, or overnight. The next day, drain and rinse well. Discard the soaking liquid.

Remove the stalks from the mushrooms and discard. Set the mushroom caps aside.

Blend the walnuts, olive oil, lime juice, water, spring onion (scallion), salt and smoked paprika in a blender or food processor until smooth.

Fill each mushroom cap with the walnut filling, then top with a little vegan pesto. Serve fresh.

CARROT & AVOCADO SUSHI ROLLS

Vegan sushi rolls are a real treat served with spicy wasabi, fresh slices of ginger and gluten-free tamari or soy sauce. You will need a sushi-rolling mat to create the perfect roll.

Makes 12 sushi rolls

For the riced carrot

2 carrots, peeled and diced

pinch mineral salt

2 tsp rice wine vinegar

For the sushi rolls

2 untoasted nori seaweed sheets

¼ red onion, peeled and sliced

¼ avocado, peeled, pitted and sliced

¼ yellow (bell) pepper, sliced

1 large tomato, seeded and sliced

small handful coriander (cilantro) leaves

To serve

1 cm/½ inch piece ginger, peeled and very finely
   sliced wasabi

tamari or gluten-free soy sauce

To make the riced carrot, process all the ingredients in a food processor until it is a similar texture to rice.

To make the sushi rolls, lay a sushi rolling mat out on a flat surface with the short edge of the mat facing you. Place 1 nori sheet on top of the mat, then spread half the riced carrot evenly onto the nori sheet, leaving the 2.5 cm/1 inch strip of nori nearest to you uncovered.

Using half the ingredients, place the sliced onion in a single line on top of the riced carrot, then place a line of sliced avocado next to the onion, followed by a line of yellow (bell) pepper, then a line of tomato topped with coriander (cilantro) leaves.

Dampen the uncovered 2.5 cm/1 inch nori strip with a little water, then starting from the far edge of the mat, carefully roll up the sushi mat towards you, making sure that the roll is tight. Press the roll down onto the dampened nori to seal.

Using a very sharp dampened knife, cut the sushi roll into 6 pieces, then repeat with the second half of the ingredients. Serve with ginger, wasabi and tamari or soy sauce.

Note

If you don't feel confident about making sushi rolls, check online for a good sushi rolling method video.

GUACAMOLE

A Mexican favourite, guacamole is a naturally raw dish. Serve with crudités or slices of tomato for a fresh, light bite, or pile it onto a salad for a main meal.

Makes 1 medium bowl

2 avocados, peeled and pitted

½ red onion, peeled and finely diced

juice of 1 lime

1 tomato, finely diced

¼ tsp mineral salt

½ green chilli, finely diced

1 tbsp finely chopped coriander (cilantro)

raw vegetable crudités, to serve

Mash the avocados with a fork or potato masher in a bowl, then add the remaining ingredients and stir to combine. Serve with raw vegetable crudités.

CASHEW MAYONNAISE

This plant-based mayonnaise is surprisingly delicious as well as nutritious. Its rich creaminess is the perfect complement to fresh, raw vegetables. Use it anywhere you would use traditional mayonnaise, for a healthy alternative.

Makes 1 small bowl

100 ml/3½ fl oz/⅓ cup water

1 spring onion (scallion), cut into slices

1 tbsp lemon juice

150 g/5 oz/1 cup cashew nuts

pinch mineral salt

Blend all the ingredients together in a blender or food processor until smooth.

Cashew mayonnaise will last 24 hours in an airtight container in the refrigerator.

Note

If you are using a stick blender, soften the cashews by soaking them in water for 2–4 hours before using. This will give a creamier mayonnaise.

VEGAN PESTO

Pesto is usually made with Parmesan, but you will not miss the cheese in this recipe. Freshly made pesto is far superior in taste to shop-bought pesto, and takes minutes to make. Serve with raw or gluten-free pasta or as a dip with raw vegetable crudités.

Serves 2 with pasta

2 spring onions (scallions)

75 g/3 oz/½ cup pine nuts

1 bunch basil leaves

½ tsp mineral salt

2 tbsp extra virgin olive oil

1 tsp balsamic vinegar

2 tbsp water

Cut off the dark green leaves of the spring onions (scallions) and discard. Roughly chop the remaining spring onions (scallions).

Blend all the ingredients together in a blender or food processor to make a chunky paste. Serve.

If saving for later, pesto can be stored in an airtight container in the refrigerator for up to 3 days, or in the freezer for up to a month.

RAW KETCHUP

Sun-dried tomatoes give this raw ketchup a delicious depth of flavour that works well on spiralized vegetables and cooked gluten-free pasta. Use it anywhere as a fresh and healthy alternative to traditional ketchup.

Makes approximately 1 x 250 ml/8 fl oz/1 cup jar

3 tomatoes

3 tbsp extra virgin olive oil

2 tsp lemon juice

6 sun-dried tomato halves, rehydrated or in oil

1 garlic clove, peeled

½ tsp mineral salt

2 Medjool dates, pitted

1 tsp thyme

1 tsp rosemary

1 tbsp basil

Blend all the ingredients together in a blender or food processor until you have a smooth ketchup-like paste.

Store in an airtight container in the refrigerator for up to 5 days, or in the freezer for up to a month.

SALADS & DRESSINGS

LEMON & GARLIC DRESSING

This deceptively simple dressing is a sophisticated twist on a traditional vinaigrette. It works with pretty much any kind of salad, and can also be used as a dip.

Makes enough for 1 large salad

1 garlic clove, peeled and crushed
100 ml/3½ fl oz/⅓ cup extra virgin olive oil
juice and zest of ½ lemon
¼ tsp mineral salt

Mix all the ingredients together thoroughly in a bowl before tossing with fresh salad.

Store in an airtight container in the refrigerator for up to 4 days.

AVOCADO DRESSING

A creamy raw dressing is a must-have for your recipe repertoire. Avocado is incredibly good for you and its natural richness works well with leafy salads, coleslaws and as a dip for crudités.

Makes enough for 1 large salad

½ medium avocado, peeled and pitted
150 ml/2 fl oz/¼ cup water
juice of 1 lime
handful basil leaves
1 spring onion (scallion), chopped
large pinch mineral salt

Blend all the ingredients together in a blender or food processor until smooth and creamy. Serve.

If saving for later, store in an airtight container in the refrigerator for up to 2 days.

CELERIAC CARPACCIO
with Herbs & Peas

Salads do not need to be simple. This gorgeous dish makes a lovely starter (appetizer). Here we use celeriac (celery root), but you can also use other firm vegetables, such as beetroot (beet) or squash.

Serves 2 as a main dish or 4 as a starter (appetizer)

For the carpaccio

1 large celeriac (celery root), peeled and cut into very fine slices
juice of 1 lemon
¼ tsp mineral salt

For the herbs & peas

75 g/3 oz/½ cup peas, fresh, or defrosted if frozen
30 g/1 oz/1 cup parsley leaves
10 g/¼ oz/½ cup tarragon leaves
50 g/2 oz/⅓ cup sunflower seeds

For the dressing

50 ml/2 fl oz/¼ cup extra virgin olive oil
1 tsp raw honey or raw agave syrup

To make the carpaccio marinade, place the celeriac (celery root) slices in a bowl, with the lemon juice and salt and toss until the celeriac is coated all over. Set aside.

For the herbs and peas, mix the peas, parsley and tarragon leaves together in a bowl.

Drain the celeriac (celery root), reserving the marinade for the dressing and blot the celeriac (celery root) with kitchen paper (paper towels).

To make the dressing, combine 1 tablespoon of the celeriac (celery root) marinade with the olive oil and honey or agave syrup. Toss the peas, parsley and tarragon into the dressing.

Divide the celeriac (celery root) carpaccio slices between 2 or 4 plates, top with the peas and herbs mixture and finish with a sprinkling of sunflower seeds.

CARROT CRISP SALAD

The carrot crisp in this salad adds another dimension. You will need a dehydrator to make the carrot crisp, but if you don't have a dehydrator, just use finely sliced carrot instead.

Serves 1 as a main dish or 3 as a side

3 carrots, peeled and finely sliced

1 tbsp melted extra virgin coconut oil

1 tsp mineral salt

1 quantity lemon & garlic dressing (*see* page 154)

1 basil sprig, to garnish

For the salad

handful rocket (arugula)

3 generous handfuls shredded lettuce

6 cherry tomatoes, sliced

handful chopped walnuts

handful shredded basil

Toss the carrot slices, coconut oil and salt together in a bowl. Lay a dehydrator greaseproof (wax) sheet onto a dehydrator tray. Spread out the carrot slices on the greaseproof sheet and dehydrate at 45°C/113°F for 6–8 hours until crisp.

Toss all the salad ingredients together in a bowl. Drizzle over the dressing, then scatter over the carrot crisps and finish with a sprig of basil.

ZINGY SUMMER TANGERINE SALAD

Fruit is not often used in savoury salads, but their sweet freshness contrasts beautifully with strong salad flavours like spring onion (scallion), as well as with the mellow flavours of cucumber and salad leaves.

Serves 1 as a main dish or 3 as a side

2 tangerines, peeled and cut into segments

⅓ lettuce, roughly chopped

⅓ cucumber, diced

2 spring onions (scallions), sliced

2 handfuls roughly chopped pecan nuts

For the dressing

juice of 2 tangerines

1 tsp unpasteurized apple cider vinegar

150 ml/¼ pint/⅔ cup extra virgin olive oil

1 tsp raw honey or raw agave syrup

large pinch mineral salt

Mix all the dressing ingredients together thoroughly in a bowl and set aside.

Cut off the inner and outer edges of each tangerine segment with a sharp knife, discarding the segment membranes so you are left with just the inner tangerine flesh and put into a large bowl. Add the remaining salad ingredients and toss together.

Add the dressing just before serving.

SPINACH, TOMATO & PEPPER
Spicy Salad

The colours of this salad will make your mouth water, while the chilli gives it a kick. This is a lovely dish for any time of year, and it looks particularly good as part of a summer picnic.

Serves 1 as a main dish or 3 as a side

3 handfuls baby leaf spinach

1 tomato, cut into slices

½ yellow (bell) pepper, seeded and sliced

½ large red chilli, seeded and finely sliced

¼ small red onion, peeled and finely sliced

handful pitted Kalamata olives

For the dressing

100 ml/3½ fl oz/⅓ cup extra virgin olive oil

1 tbsp balsamic vinegar

pinch mineral salt

Mix all the dressing ingredients together thoroughly in a bowl and set aside.

Toss all the salad ingredients together in a bowl.

Add the dressing just before serving.

COURGETTE, PUMPKIN & CABBAGE
Seasonal Salad

This hearty autumn (fall) salad is surprisingly filling. It is a great one to take to work as a packed lunch, or as a quick midday meal. If you can't find pumpkin, carrot works well too.

Serves 1 as a main dish or 3 as a side

½ courgette (zucchini), peeled and julienned

140 g/5 oz/1 cup pumpkin, peeled, seeded and julienned

55 g/2 oz/1 cup white cabbage, shredded

¼ red (bell) pepper, seeded and sliced

¼ yellow (bell) pepper, seeded and sliced

10 g/¼ oz/¼ cup finely chopped parsley

1 quantity lemon & garlic dressing (*see* page 154)

Toss all the ingredients together in a bowl with the dressing.

If left to marinate for a few hours, the dressing will soften the vegetables. If you prefer your vegetables to be crunchy, dress the salad just before serving.

SIMPLE AVOCADO SALAD

Avocados are one of the best raw foods for transitioning away from cooked foods as they replenish the body with essential oils and other nutrients. If you like them, eating an avocado a day will do you wonders.

Serves 1 as a main dish or 3 as a side

1 avocado, peeled, pitted and diced

10 cherry tomatoes, cut in half

1 small carrot, peeled and sliced

handful basil leaves

2 tbsp extra virgin olive oil

large pinch mineral salt

Toss all the ingredients together in a bowl. Serve immediately.

CARROT SALAD

The texture of spiralized vegetables always looks great in a salad. In this dish, the sweetness of the pears and carrots is complemented by the mustardy heat of the dressing.

Serves 1 as a main dish or 3 as a side

1 small pear, cored and thinly sliced

4 handfuls rocket (arugula)

2 medium carrots, spiralized or julienned

2 small handfuls cashew nuts

2 small handfuls dried cranberries

For the dressing

100 ml/3½ fl oz/⅓ cup extra virgin olive oil

1 tbsp unpasteurized apple cider vinegar

2 tsp Dijon mustard

1 tsp raw honey or raw agave syrup

pinch mineral salt

2 pinches freshly ground black pepper

Mix all the dressing ingredients together thoroughly in a bowl and set aside.

Arrange the salad in layers, starting with the pear slices, then the rocket (arugula) and carrots.

Finish by sprinkling over the cashews and cranberries before adding the dressing. Serve.

SOUPS & MAIN MEALS

COURGETTE SPAGHETTI
with Walnut Pesto

This recipe is a twist on a raw food favourite, as it combines courgette spaghetti with the earthy richness of walnuts and the fresh flavours of basil for an alternative vegan pesto.

Makes enough for 2

3 courgettes (zucchini)

8 cherry tomatoes, cut in half

For the pesto

50 g/2 oz/½ cup walnuts

25 g/1 oz/1 cup basil leaves

1 chopped whole spring onion (scallion)

1 tbsp lemon juice

¼ tsp mineral salt

2 tbsp nutritional yeast flakes

1 tbsp extra virgin olive oil

To make the pesto, soak the walnuts in water for 8 hours, or overnight.

The next day, drain the walnuts and put them into a small food processor with the remaining pesto ingredients. Blitz until relatively smooth.

Use a spiralizer or julienne peeler to make the courgette (zucchini) spaghetti.

Place the spaghetti, pesto and cherry tomatoes in a large bowl and mix together before serving.

VEGGIE PIZZA
on a Sprouted Buckwheat & Flaxseed Crust

This delicious pizza is a showstopper when it comes to introducing friends to raw food. Alternatively, snuggle up on the sofa for pizza and a movie, raw style.

Makes one 30 cm/12 inch or two 15 cm/6 inch pizzas

For the pizza base

80 g/3 oz/½ cup ground flaxseed

140 g/5 oz/1¼ cups red (bell) pepper, chopped

250 g/9 oz/1½ cups raw buckwheat, sprouted for 24 hours

pinch mineral salt

1 tbsp dried oregano

1 garlic clove, chopped

1 quantity vegan pesto (*see* page 149)

For the topping

6 chestnut (cremini) mushrooms, sliced

½ courgette (zucchini), sliced

1 red (bell) pepper, cored, seeded and chopped

½ medium red onion, peeled and sliced

3 tbsp extra virgin olive oil

large pinch mineral salt

For the almond 'Parmesan'

40 g/1½ oz/¼ cup whole raw almonds

1 garlic clove, peeled and crushed

1 tbsp lemon juice

¼ tsp mineral salt

Place the pizza base ingredients, except the pesto, in a food processor and process until smooth. Using a spatula, spread the pizza base mixture onto a dehydrator greaseproof (wax) sheet to make 1 large pizza circle or 2 smaller pizza circles.

Dehydrate the pizza base at 45°C/113°F for 4 hours. Remove the dehydrator sheet and place the pizza base back onto the mesh shelves of your dehydrator for a further 12 hours.

Mix all the topping ingredients together in a bowl. Spread the mixture onto another dehydrator sheet and dehydrate at 45°C/113°F for 2–4 hours until warm and slightly softened.

To make the almond cheese, mix all the ingredients together in a food processor until crumbly in texture. Set aside.

Spread the vegan pesto evenly over the pizza base, top with dehydrated vegetables and sprinkle over the almond cheese before serving.

CUPCAKE QUICHE

Serve up these savoury cupcakes as a real treat for a romantic dinner or for when you have friends round. Don't be fooled by their size; they are surprisingly satisfying.

Makes 6 cupcakes

For the cases (shells)

2 large carrots, peeled and sliced

130 g/4½ oz/1 cup ground flaxseed

300 g/11 oz/2 cups Brazil nuts

70 g/2½ oz/½ cup sunflower seeds

½ tsp sea salt

1 garlic clove, peeled

1 tbsp water (optional)

For the filling

1 cup sunflower seeds, soaked for 4-8 hours and rinsed

juice of 1 lemon

2 tbsp extra virgin olive oil

110 g/4 oz/1 cup sun-dried tomatoes

50 ml/2 fl oz/¼ cup water

1 tbsp nutritional yeast flakes

1 tbsp oregano leaves

¼ tsp mineral salt

To garnish

3 cherry tomatoes, sliced

1 tbsp chopped parsley

1 tbsp dehydrated onion, optional

Using a cupcake tin, oil 6 of the cupcake sections with olive oil.

Blitz all the ingredients for the cases (shells) in a food processor until well processed and sticking together. Add the water if the mixture is not sticking.

Divide the pastry mixture evenly into 6 portions and, using clean hands, press the mixture into the oiled cupcake sections until each case (shell) is about 5 mm/½ inch thick.

Place the cupcake tin in the dehydrator and dehydrate at 45°C/113°F for 4–5 hours until set. Carefully remove the dehydrated cupcake cases (shells) from the cupcake tin and set aside.

Place all the ingredients for the filling in a food processor and process until creamy. Fill each case (shell) with the filling.

Garnish with cherry tomatoes, parsley and onion, if using, and serve with salad.

VEGGIE PESTO WRAP

Raw wraps are great to make in bulk, as they freeze very well. To defrost them, take them out of the freezer a couple of hours before you want to use them.

Makes 2 wraps

For the wraps

200 g/7 oz/2 cups diced courgette (zucchini)

90 g/3 oz/3 cups spinach

3 tbsp extra virgin olive oil

2 tsp lemon juice

pinch cayenne pepper

1 tsp ground coriander

½ tsp mineral salt

65 g/2½ oz/½ cup ground flaxseeds

For the filling

vegan pesto (*see* page 149) or your choice of dip or sauce, e.g. guacamole (*see* page 144), cashew mayonnaise (*see* page 146), ketchup (*see* page 150); mixed sliced vegetables of your choice, such as (bell) peppers, cucumber, onion, courgette (zucchini) and mushrooms.

To make the wraps, blend the courgette (zucchini), spinach, olive oil and lemon juice together in a blender or food processor until smooth. Add the spices, salt and flaxseeds and blend thoroughly to combine.

Spread the wrap mixture into two 20 cm/8 inch circles on 2 dehydrator trays with greaseproof (wax) sheets and dehydrate at 45°C/113°F for 8 hours. Remove the dehydrator sheets and place the wraps back onto the mesh shelves of your dehydrator and dehydrate for a further 30–60 minutes, so that the wraps are still pliable.

Use the dehydrated wraps immediately or store them in an airtight container in the refrigerator for up to 48 hours, or freeze them for up to a month.

To make the veggie wraps, spread a generous line of vegan pesto or your chosen spread along one end of the wrap and lay the vegetables on top of the spread. Starting with the filled end, roll your wrap closed. Serve edge-down with salad.

AUBERGINE & PESTO TERRINE

Preserved aubergine (eggplant) is a delicious raw antipasti. It needs a little forward planning, as it takes a week to preserve and to be ready to use in this recipe. Sterilize your preserving jar by washing it in a dishwasher or by placing it in a hot oven for 10 minutes.

Makes 1 x 500 ml/18 fl oz jar to serve 4

For the preserved aubergine

3 large aubergines (eggplants), cut into 1 cm/½ inch slices

4 tbsp mineral salt

250 ml/8 fl oz/1 cup unpasteurized apple cider vinegar

small bunch basil leaves

3 garlic cloves, peeled and thinly sliced

200 ml/7 fl oz/¾ cup extra virgin olive oil

For the terrine

oil, for oiling

4 tomatoes, quartered and seeded

1 orange (bell) pepper, halved and seeded

1 large courgette (zucchini), trimmed and cut lengthways into 4 slices

2 quantities vegan pesto (*see* page 149)

basil leaves, to garnish

To make the preserved aubergine (eggplant), toss the aubergine (eggplant) slices with the salt. Put the slices in a colander inside a large bowl and drain for at least 12 hours, then press as much of the remaining liquid out of the aubergine (eggplant) as you can.

Thoroughly mix the drained aubergine (eggplant) with the vinegar and leave for 1–2 hours.

Pack the aubergine (eggplant) into a large, sterilized preserving jar, layering with the basil and garlic slices as you go. Press the aubergine (eggplant) down, draining off any excess vinegar, until the jar is full.

Fill the jar to the top with olive oil before sealing, then leave in the refrigerator for at least a week.

For the terrine, lightly oil a 500 g/1 lb 2 oz loaf tin with olive oil. Flatten the tomato quarters and orange (bell) pepper halves with your hand.

Blot the preserved aubergine (eggplant) slices with kitchen paper (paper towels), then use to cover the base and sides of the tin. Layer the ingredients, starting with a portion of pesto, then 8 tomato quarters, aubergine (eggplant) slices, 2 courgette (zucchini) slices, orange (bell) peppers, 8 tomato quarters, a portion pesto, aubergine (eggplant) slices and finishing with 2 courgette (zucchini) slices.

Cover the top of the terrine with clingfilm (plastic wrap), lay weights (e.g. food cans or jars containing water) on top and leave the terrine to compress in the refrigerator for at least 4 hours.

Garnish with basil to serve.

CLASSIC GAZPACHO

Gazpacho is a savoury summer delight. If you do not have time to chill the ingredients, then add a few ice cubes as you blend. Serve in glasses for an added touch of sophistication.

Makes 1 large bowl or 4 glasses

1 red (bell) pepper, seeded

½ cucumber

8 tomatoes, seeded and roughly chopped

¼ small red onion, peeled and roughly chopped

50 ml/2 fl oz/¼ cup extra virgin olive oil

juice of ½ lime

4 ice cubes

½ jalapeño chilli, seeded

2 tbsp basil leaves

½ tsp mineral salt

large pinch ground black pepper

basil leaves, to garnish

For the garnish, cut 2 slices of red (bell) pepper, dice them and set aside in a bowl. Cut 2 thick slices of cucumber, dice and add to the bowl.

Blend all the remaining ingredients in a blender or food processor until smooth.

Serve immediately, topped with reserved diced red (bell) pepper, diced cucumber and some basil leaves.

BEETROOT GAZPACHO

The colour of this soup inevitably elicits appreciation, in anticipation of its fresh and fruity flavours. Serve it in a big bowl as a hearty lunch or in smaller glasses as an elegant starter (appetizer).

Makes 1 large bowl or 4 glasses

½ cucumber, peeled

1 red apple, cored

1 beetroot (beet)

125 ml/4 fl oz/½ cup freshly squeezed orange juice (about 2 oranges)

4 ice cubes

1 red (bell) pepper, cored and seeded

50 ml/2 fl oz/¼ cup extra virgin olive oil

1 garlic clove, peeled and crushed

½ tsp mineral salt

For the garnish, cut 1 thick slice of cucumber, dice it and put it in a bowl. Dice half the apple and add it to the garnish bowl. If you are lucky enough to have some baby beetroot (beet) leaves, add a few of these to your garnish bowl too. Set aside.

Place the orange juice in a blender with the remaining ingredients and blend until smooth.

Serve garnished with the cucumber, apple and baby beetroot (beet) leaves if you have them.

Note

If you are using a stick blender, grate the beetroot (beet) first.

CARROT SOUP

This warming soup is just as satisfying as its cooked brethren and so much better for you. Warm your bowls before serving so that the soup keeps its heat for longer.

Makes 1 large or 2 medium bowls

100 ml/3½ fl oz/⅓ cup raw almond milk (*see* page 88)

3 medium carrots, peeled

handful parsley, plus extra to garnish

½ small garlic clove

1 tsp ground cumin

1 tsp ground coriander

1 cm/½ inch piece ginger, peeled

½ tsp mineral salt

200 ml/7 fl oz/¾ cup just-boiled water

Set 2 tablespoon of almond milk aside, then add the rest to a blender with the remaining ingredients and blitz until smooth and creamy. Pour into bowls.

Drizzle with the reserved almond milk, top with a parsley sprig and serve.

Note

If you are using a stick blender, grate the carrots first.

SWEET TREATS

RED BERRY CHEESECAKE

Raw cheesecakes are magic. They are one of the best ways to
impress friends and show them what raw food is all about. Not only
does this red berry cheesecake taste utterly delicious, it looks
gorgeous too.

Makes enough for 12 slices

For the base

40 g/1½ oz/½ cup desiccated (dried unsweetened) coconut,
  plus extra to decorate
75 g/3 oz/½ cup macadamia nuts
pinch mineral salt
2 tbsp raw honey or raw agave syrup
50 ml/2 fl oz/¼ cup melted extra virgin coconut oil

For the filling

300 g/11 oz/2 cups red berries
125 ml/4 fl oz/½ cup water
50 ml/2 fl oz/¼ cup raw agave syrup
125 ml/4 fl oz/½ cup melted extra virgin coconut oil
225 g/8 oz/1½ cups cashew nuts
1 tsp nutritional yeast flakes
pinch mineral salt

Sprinkle a small handful of the dessicated coconut onto the base
of an 18 cm/7 in loose-bottomed cake tin.

Place the remaining ingredients for the base in a food processor and blitz until combined. Press the mixture evenly on top of the coconut in the tin.

For the filling, blend the berries, then strain into a bowl. Set aside 50 ml/2 fl oz/¼ cup purée.

Put the remaining berry purée into a blender, add the rest of the filling ingredients and blend until smooth. Spread the filling on top of the cheesecake base.

Pour over the reserved berry purée, gently shaking the tin to spread it out, then leave to set in the refrigerator to set for 2–4 hours.

To serve, release the base of the cake tin and slide the cheesecake onto a plate. Top with a sprinkle of coconut.

DATE, CHOCOLATE & WALNUT BARS

These walnut chocolate bars are great for taking on picnics or to work for a mid-afternoon snack. Make them at the weekend so you have a stack of them to last the week.

Makes 12 bars

100 g/3½ oz/1 cup walnuts

170 g/6 oz/1 cup Medjool dates, pitted

50 g/2 oz/½ cup raw cacao powder

pinch mineral salt

2 tsp vanilla extract

50 ml/2 fl oz/¼ cup melted cacao butter or extra virgin coconut oil

Roughly chop the walnuts in a food processor. Add the remaining ingredients and process until thoroughly combined, occasionally stopping the machine to push the mixture into the blades before continuing.

Put the mixture onto a large, square sheet of baking parchment and press the mixture into a square, about 1 cm/½ inch deep. Use a large knife to keep the edges straight.

Using a sharp knife, cut the mixture into 12 bars. Store in an airtight container in the refrigerator for up to 5 days or in the freezer for up to 1 month.

CHIA PUDDING
with Strawberries

Chia seeds are a delicious way of getting omega oils into your diet, which are good for your joints, brain and heart. This light milky dessert hits the spot when it comes to summer puddings.

Makes 4

75 g/3 oz/½ cup chia seeds
400 ml/14 fl oz/1⅔ cups raw almond milk (*see* page 88)
½ tsp vanilla extract
½ tsp stevia powder
28 strawberries

Combine the chia seeds, almond milk, vanilla extract and ¼ teaspoon stevia powder in a jug. Stir every 5 minutes for 30 minutes to avoid clumping.

Meawhile, cut 12 of the strawberries in half and use to line the base of 4 glasses.

After 30 minutes, carefully pour the chia pudding on top of the strawberries, making sure you leave enough room for the strawberry coulis on top.

Blend the remaining strawberries with the rest of the stevia powder in a blender until smooth. Divide the strawberry coulis between the glasses.

Cover each glass with clingfilm (plastic wrap) and leave to set in the refrigerator for at least 2 hours before serving.

COCONUT BARS

These lovely, fresh bars are great to make in batch. Best kept in the freezer, you will have a sweet treat available whenever the need calls. Use brown coconuts rather than green ones for the fresh coconut.

Makes 12 bars

250 g/9 oz grated fresh coconut or frozen fresh coconut (found in Asian supermarkets)
1 tsp vanilla extract
1 tbsp xylitol
150 ml/¼ pint/⅔ cup melted extra virgin coconut oil
pinch mineral salt

Line a shallow tin, about 15 x 12 cm/6 x 5 inches with clingfilm (plastic wrap).

Mix all the ingredients together thoroughly in a mixing bowl, then press the mixture into the prepared tin, compressing it with your fingers.

Place the tin in the freezer for 1–2 hours.

Remove the tin from the freezer. Lift the set coconut bar mixture from the tin and remove the clingfilm (plastic wrap). Using a hot, sharp knife, slice into 12 bars.

Store the coconut bars in an airtight container in the freezer for up to 1 month.

LIME CHEESECAKE

Fresh and zingy, this raw cheesecake is perfect as a dessert or for afternoon tea.
If you have any leftovers, cut the remaining cheesecake into slices before wrapping
and freezing each slice individually.

Makes enough for 12 slices

For the base

95 g/3 oz/1 cup freshly ground raw almonds

¼ tsp mineral salt

85 g/3 oz/½ cup Medjool dates, pitted and finely chopped

For the centre

225 g/8 oz/1½ cups cashew nuts

grated zest of 2 limes

50 ml/2 fl oz/¼ cup lime juice

50 ml/2 fl oz/¼ cup melted extra virgin coconut oil

100 ml/3½ fl oz/⅓ cup water

2 tbsp vanilla extract

½ tsp nutritional yeast flakes

For the topping

75 g/3 oz/½ cup cashew nuts

zest of 2 limes, plus extra to decorate

50 ml/2 fl oz/¼ cup lime juice

1 tbsp melted extra virgin coconut oil

¼ tsp spirulina powder

Sprinkle a small handful of the ground almonds onto the base of an 18 cm/7 inch loose-bottomed cake tin.

Place the remaining almonds into a bowl, add the salt and dates and knead together to form a dough. Using wet hands, press the dough into the base of the cake tin. Set aside.

Blend the ingredients for the centre together in a blender until smooth, then pour onto the cheesecake base.

Optional: to create the decorative green indentation in the cheesecake, push the edge of the spatula down at an angle about 2.5 cm/1 inch from the edge of the cake tin, and draw a 'ditch' around the cake at this angle.

Blend the topping ingredients together, then spread on top of the filling with a spatula, filling the ditch with topping.

Leave to set in the refrigerator for 2–4 hours.

Release the base of the cake tin and slide the cheesecake onto a plate. Decorate with lime zest.

CHOCOLATE COOKIES
with Buckwheat

Buckwheaties can be used in many different ways. In this recipe, they add crunch and lightness to these cookies. Use a dehydrator to make your own buckwheaties, or you can buy them online or in your local health food shop.

Makes 8–10

125 g/4 oz/⅔ cup raw buckwheat, soaked and sprouted for 24 hours

For the cookies

50 g/2 oz/½ cup raw cacao powder, plus extra for dusting (optional)
2 tsp ground cinnamon
250 g/9 oz/1½ cups raisins
1 tsp vanilla extract
pinch mineral salt

To make the buckwheaties, spread the sprouted buckwheat onto a dehydrator greaseproof (wax) sheet and dehydrate at 45°C/113°F for 8–12 hours until thoroughly dried out.

To make the cookies, combine the cacao powder, cinnamon, raisins, vanilla extract and salt in a food processor. Transfer to a bowl and stir through the buckwheaties.

Put the cookie mixture onto a large piece of baking parchment and press the mixture flat so it is slightly less than 1 cm/½ inch thick. Use a large knife to keep the edges straight.

Cut the cookie mixture into squares or rectangles, then dust with extra cacao powder, if using.

FRUIT LEATHER

Fruit leathers are super-simple to make in a dehydrator. You can literally use any fruit to make fruit leather, so experiment to find your favourite. They make great healthy snacks for kids.

Makes 2 dehydrator trays

500 g/1 lb 2 oz/3 cups plums, pitted
500 g/1 lb 2 oz/3 cups apples, cored
2 ripe bananas, peeled or 2 tbsp raw honey

Blend the plums, apples and bananas or honey together in a blender or food processor until smooth. If the plums are not juicy, add a little water to help with blending.

Spread the fruit purée onto dehydrator greaseproof (wax) sheets to about 5 mm/¼ inch thick. Leave a 2.5 cm/1 inch gap around the edge to allow for spreading.

Dehydrate at 45°C/113°F for 3 hours. Peel off the dehydrator sheets and return the fruit leather to the mesh shelves of the dehydrator and dry for a further 5 hours. They are ready when finger pressure does not leave a mark and the fruit leather feels dry.

When the fruit leather has cooled, cut it into strips. Roll up and store in an airtight container in the dark. Eat within a month or freeze them for up to 6 months.

CHOCOLATE ALMOND LAYER CAKE

This sophisticated dessert is a great dinner party addition. It can be made in advance to save on time and keeps well covered in the refrigerator for a few days.

Makes 2

For the almond layer

95 g/3 oz/1 cup freshly ground almonds

pinch mineral salt

50 ml/2 fl oz/¼ cup melted extra virgin coconut oil

50 ml/2 fl oz/¼ cup raw honey or raw agave syrup

For the chocolate layer

50 g/2 oz/¼ cup raw cacao butter

2 tbsp extra virgin coconut oil

50 g/2 oz/¼ cup Medjool dates, pitted, soaked and drained

100 g/3½ oz/1 cup raw cacao powder

2 tsp vanilla extract

125 ml/4 fl oz/½ cup raw honey or raw agave syrup

pinch mineral salt

strawberries, to decorate

Combine all the almond layer ingredients together in a bowl.

Using four 8 cm/3 inch chef's rings, press down a quarter of the almond mixture into the base of each ring and leave to set in the refrigerator for 2 hours.

For the chocolate layer, melt the cacao butter and coconut oil in a heatproof bowl set over a pan of gently simmering water. Make sure the base of the bowl doesn't touch the water.

Transfer the melted butter and oil to a blender or food processor, add the remaining ingredients and blend until thick and smooth. If the mixture is too thick, add 1 tablespoon water at a time.

Spoon a quarter of the chocolate mixture into each ring, smoothing the top, then carefully remove the cake layers from the rings, pushing them up from the bottom.

Double up the chocolate and almond layers to make 2 cakes. Decorate with strawberries before serving.

Note

If you don't have chef's rings, use round glasses lined with clingfilm (plastic wrap) instead.

BANANA & CASHEW OAT BARS

This super-simple recipe takes minutes to make. A favourite of children, the oats release their energy slowly, so this is also a great breakfast substitute if you find yourself dashing out of the door in a hurry.

Makes 6

3 large bananas, peeled

1 tbsp lemon juice

150 g/5 oz/1 cup cashew nuts

200 g/7 oz/2 cups rolled oats

pinch mineral salt

50 ml/2 fl oz/¼ cup melted extra virgin coconut oil

Line a 20 x 15 cm/8 x 6 inch shallow tray with clingfilm (plastic wrap).

Mash the bananas and lemon juice together by hand or in a blender.

Process the cashews and oats in a food processor until finely chopped. Add the salt, banana purée and coconut oil and process until well combined.

Using a spatula, press the mixture into the prepared tray until it is flat. Cover and leave to set in the refrigerator for 1 hour.

When set, remove the banana and cashew oat mixture from the tin, uncover and, using a sharp knife, cut into 6 bars.

Eat fresh or store in an airtight container in the freezer for up to a month.

CARROT CAKE

This raw take on the classic carrot cake is super-fresh and light. The frosting and jewel-coloured cranberries give it an extra special feel, making it a great choice for birthdays and special occasions.

Makes enough for 12 slices

4 large carrots, peeled and grated

200 g/7 oz/1¼ cups almonds

50 g/2 oz/scant ½ cup dried cranberries

2 tsp ground cinnamon

50 ml/2 fl oz/¼ cup raw honey or raw agave syrup

1 tsp vanilla extract

grated zest of ½ orange

For the frosting

200 g/7 oz/1⅓ cups cashew nuts

1 tsp nutritional yeast flakes

1 tsp vanilla extract

zest and juice of 1 lemon

50 ml/2 fl oz/¼ cup melted extra virgin coconut oil

3 tbsp water

2 tbsp raw honey or raw agave syrup

To decorate

chopped dried cranberries

chopped cashew nuts

Line an 18 cm/7 inch springform cake tin with clingfilm (plastic wrap).

Combine all the cake ingredients in a food processor until the almonds are chopped into small pieces.

Blend all the frosting ingredients together until creamy and smooth.

Spoon half the cake mixture into the prepared tin and flatten down with the back of a spoon. Spoon half the frosting mixture into the tin and smooth over with a spatula. Repeat the process for the final 2 layers.

Decorate with chopped cranberries and cashews and chill for 2–4 hours before serving.

CHOCOLATE TRUFFLES

Little balls of fudgy deliciousness, what more could you want when you get that sweet craving? Made with whole, dried fruits to sweeten them, these truffles are a chocolate-caramel flavour sensation.

Makes 15

130 g/4½ oz/1 cup soft prunes
170 g/6 oz/1 cup Medjool dates, pitted
50 ml/2 fl oz/¼ cup melted extra virgin coconut oil
100 g/3½ oz/1 cup raw cacao powder
2 tsp vanilla extract
pinch mineral salt

To finish

desiccated (dried unsweetened) coconut
raw cacao powder

Process all the truffle ingredients together in a food processor until smooth.

Put the coconut on a small plate and the cacao powder on another.

Roll approximately 1 tablespoon of truffle mixture between the palms of your hands to make a 2.5 cm/1 inch ball. Continue until the mixture is used up.

To finish, roll half the truffle balls through the cacao powder and half through the coconut until coated. Leave to set in the refrigerator for 2–4 hours.

TROPICAL CUPCAKES

Xylitol is used to sweeten the filling in these cupcakes. It has a neutral flavour that works well with fruit and its white colour keeps the natural shades of the mango and passion fruit clear and fresh.

Makes 6

For the cases (shells)

90 g/3 oz/½ cup soft unsulphured dried apricots

150 g/5 oz/1 cup macadamia nuts

50 ml/2 fl oz/¼ cup melted extra virgin coconut oil

For the filling

100 g/3½ oz/½ cup fresh brown coconut, brown skin removed

50 g/2 oz/½ cup ripe mango, peeled and stoned

grated zest of 1 lime

juice of ½ lime

1 tbsp xylitol

50 ml/2 fl oz/¼ cup melted extra virgin coconut oil

3 passion fruit

Line 6 sections of a cupcake tin with clingfilm (plastic wrap).

For the cases (shells), process the dried apricots with the macadamia nuts and coconut oil in a food processor until a smooth dough forms.

Press the dough evenly over the base and sides of the prepared cupcake sections and leave to set in the freezer while you make the filling.

Blend the fresh coconut, mango, lime zest and juice, xylitol and coconut oil in a blender until smooth.

Spoon a generous amount of filling into each set cupcake case (shell) and put in the refrigerator to set for 1–2 hours.

Before serving, remove the cupcakes from the tin. Cut the passion fruit in half, scoop out the seeds and spoon them onto the tops of the cupcakes.

NUTTY CHOCOLATE BAR

If you like nutty chocolate brownies, then you will enjoy these delicious bars. Make up batches and freeze them, ready for when friends are over or to take to a special event.

Makes 10

75 g/3 oz raw chocolate bar

115 g/4 oz/¾ cup almonds

40 g/1½ oz/¼ cup unsalted pistachios, finely chopped

75 g/3 oz/½ cup hazelnuts or filberts

90 g/3 oz/1 cup rolled oats

50 g/2 oz/½ cup raw cacao powder

pinch mineral salt

215 g/7½ oz/1¼ cups Medjool dates, pitted

2 tsp vanilla extract

2 tbsp melted raw cacao butter

Break up the raw chocolate bar and melt in a heatproof bowl set over a pan of gently simmering water, making sure the base of the bowl doesn't touch the water.

Set aside 40 g/1½ oz/¼ cup almonds and the pistachios for later.

Process the remaining nuts, the oats, cacao powder and salt in a food processor until the nuts are well chopped. Add the dates, vanilla extract and cacao butter and process until the mixture forms a dough. Place the dough on a large piece of baking parchment and flatten to make a square, about 2.5 cm/1 inch thick. Cut the square into 10 bars.

Roughly chop the remaining almonds and sprinkle on top, pressing down slightly. Using a teaspoon, drizzle over the melted chocolate and finish with a sprinkle of pistachios.

INDEX

Entries with upper-case initials indicate recipes.

If you enjoyed this book please sign up for updates,
information and offers on further titles in this series at
www.flametreepublishing.com